William Lennie

The Principles of English Grammar

William Lennie

The Principles of English Grammar

ISBN/EAN: 9783741123108

Manufactured in Europe, USA, Canada, Australia, Japa

Cover: Foto ©Andreas Hilbeck / pixelio.de

Manufactured and distributed by brebook publishing software (www.brebook.com)

William Lennie

The Principles of English Grammar

THE PRINCIPLES

OF

ENGLISH GRAMMAR:

COMPRISING

THE SUBSTANCE OF ALL THE MOST APPROVED ENGLISH
GRAMMARS EXTANT, BRIEFLY DEFINED, AND
NEATLY ARRANGED;

WITH COPIOUS

EXERCISES IN PARSING AND SYNTAX.

BY WILLIAM LENNIE,

*Teacher of English, Nicholson Street Edinburgh,
Author of "The Child's Ladder," &c.*

From the Twenty-third Edinburgh Edition.

TORONTO:
PUBLISHED BY ROBERT McPHAIL,
65 KING STREET EAST.
1863.

PREFACE.

It is probable, that the original design and principal motive of every teacher, in publishing a school-book, is the improvement of his own pupils. Such, at least, is the immediate object of the present compilation; which, for brevity of expression, neatness of arrangement, and comprehensiveness of plan, is, perhaps, superior to any other book of the kind. "My chief end has been to explain the general principles of Grammar as clearly and intelligibly as possible. In the definitions, therefore, easiness and perspicuity have been sometimes preferred to logical exactness."

Orthography is mentioned rather for the sake of order, than from a conviction of its utility; for, in my opinion, to occupy thirty or forty pages of a Grammar in defining the *sounds* of the alphabet is quite preposterous.

On Etymology I have left much to be remarked by the teacher in the time of teaching. My reason for doing this is, that children, when by themselves, labour more to have the words of their book imprinted on their memories, than to have the meaning fixed in their minds; but, on the contrary, when the teacher addresses them *viva voce*, they naturally strive rather to comprehend his meaning, than to remember his exact expressions. In pursuance of this idea, the first part of this little volume has been thrown into a form more resembling heads of Lectures on Grammar, than a complete elucidation of the subject. That the teacher, however, may not be always under the necessity of having recourse to his memory to supply the deficiencies, the most remarkable observations have been subjoined at the bottom of the page, to which the pupils themselves may occasionally be referred.

The desire of being concise has frequently induced me to use very elliptical expressions; but I trust they are all sufficiently perspicuous. I may also add, that many additional and critical remarks, which might have, with propriety, been inserted in the Grammar, have been inserted rather in the Key; for I have studiously withheld everything from the Grammar that could be spared, to keep it low-priced for the general good.

The Questions on Etymology, at the one hundred seventy-second page, will speak for themselves: they unite the advantages of both the usual methods, viz., that of plain narration, and that of question and answer, without the inconvenience of either.

Syntax is commonly divided into two parts, Concord and Government; and the rules respecting the former, grammarians in general

PREFACE.

have placed before those which relate to the latter. I have not, however, attended to this division, because I deem it of little importance; but have placed those rules first which are either more easily understood, or which more frequently occur. In arranging a number of rules, it is difficult to please every reader I have frequently been unable to satisfy myself, and, therefore, cannot expect that the arrangement which I have at last adopted will give universal satisfaction. Whatever order be preferred, the one rule must necessarily precede the other; and, since they are all to be learned, it signifies but little whether the rules of concord precede those of government, or whether they be mixed, provided no anticipations be made which may embarrass the learner.

For exercises on Syntax, I have not only selected the shortest sentences I could find, but printed the lines *closely* together, with the rules at the bottom, on a small type, and by these means have generally compressed as many faulty expressions into a single page as some of my predecessors have done into two pages of a larger size. Hence, though this book seems to contain but few exercises on bad grammar, it really contains so many, that a separate volume of exercises is quite unnecessary.

Whatever defects were found in the former edition, in the time of teaching, have been carefully supplied.

On Etymology, Syntax, Punctuation, and Prosody, there is scarcely a Rule or Observation in the largest Grammar in print that is not to be found in this; besides, the Rules and Definitions, in general, are so very short and pointed, that, compared with those in some other Grammars, they may be said to be hit off rather than made. Every page is independent, and though quite full, not crowded, but wears an air of neatness and ease invitingly sweet,—a circumstance not unimportant But, notwithstanding these properties, and others that might be mentioned, I am far from being so vain as to suppose this compilation is altogether free from inaccuracies or defects; much less do I presume that it will obtain the approbation of every one who may choose to peruse it; for, to use the words of Doctor Johnson, "He that has much to do will do something wrong, and of that wrong must suffer the consequences; and if it were possible that he should always act rightly, yet when such numbers are to judge of his conduct, the bad will censure and obstruct him by malevolence, and the good sometimes by mistake."

☞ *Those pupils that are capable of* writing, *should be requested to write the* plural of nouns, &c., *either at home or at school. The Exercises on Syntax should be written in their corrected state, with a stroke drawn* under *the word corrected.*

☞ K. means Key; the figures refer to the *No.* o. the key, the page

THE PRINCIPLES OF ENGLISH GRAMMAR.

ENGLISH GRAMMAR is the art of speaking and writing the English Language with propriety.

It is divided into four parts; namely, *Orthography, Etymology, Syntax, and Prosody.*

ORTHOGRAPHY.

ORTHOGRAPHY *teaches the nature and powers of letters, and the just method of spelling words.*

A LETTER is the least part of a Word.

There are *twenty-six* letters in English

Letters are either Vowels or Consonants.

A *Vowel* is a letter, the *name* of which makes a *full open sound* The Vowels are *a, e, i, o, u, w, y.*—The Consonants are *b, c, d, f, g, h, j, k, l, m, n, p, q, r, s, t, v, x, z.*

A Consonant is a letter that has a sound *less distinct* than that of a Vowel; as, *l, m, p.*

A *Diphthong* is the union of two vowels; as, *ou* in *out.*

A *proper* Diphthong is one in which *both* the vowels are sounded as, *oy* in *boy.*

An *improper* Diphthong is one in which only *one* of the two vowels is sounded; as, *o* in *boat.*

A *Triphthong* is the union of three vowels; as, *eau* in *beauty.*

A *Syllable* is a part of a word, or as much as can be sounded at once; as, *far* in *far-mer.*

A *Monosyllable* is a word of *one* syllable, as, *fox.*

A *Dissyllable* is a word of *two* syllables; as, *Pe-ter.*

A *Trissyllable* is a word of *three* syllables; as, *but-ter-fly.*

A *Polysyllable* is a word of *many* syllables.

☞ Why should *judgement, abridgement,* &c., be spelled without *e?* How can *g* be soft like *i* without it?—See Walker's Dictionary, under *judgement*

ETYMOLOGY.

ETYMOLOGY *treats of the different sorts of Words, their various modifications, and their derivation.*

THERE are *nine* parts of Speech: Article, Noun, Adjective, Pronoun, Verb, Adverb Preposition, Interjection, and Conjunction.

Of the ARTICLES.

An *Article* is a word put before a noun, to show the extent of its meaning; as, *a man.*

There are two articles, *a* or *an* and *the.* *A* is used before a consonant.*—*An* is used before a vowel, or silent *h;* as, *an* age, *an* hour.

Of NOUNS.

A *Noun* is the *name* of any person, place, or thing; as, *John, London, book.*

Nouns are varied, by Number, Gender, and Case

OBSERVATIONS.

* *A* is used before the long sound of *u*, and before *w* and *y*; as, A *unit,* a *euphony,* a *ewe,* a *week,* a *year,* such a *one.*—*An* is used before words beginning with *h* sounded, when the accent is on the *second* syllable; as, *An* heroic action; *an* historical account.

A is called the *indefinite* article, because it does not point out a particular person or thing; as, *A* king; that is, *any* king.

The is called the *definite* article, because it refers to a particular person, or thing; as, *The king;* that is, the king of our *own* country

A noun, without an article to limit it, is taken in its widest sense, as, *Man* is mortal; namely, *all mankind.*

A is used before nouns in the *singular* number only.—It is used before the plural in nouns preceded by such' phrases as, *A few; a great many;* as, *a few* books *a great many* apples

The is used before nouns in *both* numbers, and sometimes before adverbs in the comparative and superlative degree, as, *the more study* grammar *the better* I like it

Of Number.

Number is the distinction of *one* from *more*

Nouns have *two* numbers; the *Singular* and the *Plural*. The singular denotes *one*, the plural *more* than one.

1. The plural is generally formed by adding *s* to the singular; as, Book, books.

2. Nouns in *s*, *sh*, *ch*, *x*, or *o*, form the plural by adding *es*; as, Miss, Misses; brush, brushes; match, matches; fox, foxes; hero, heroes.—p. 10, b.*

3. Nouns in *y* change *y* into *ies* in the plural; as, Lady, ladies:—*y*, with a vowel before it, is not changed into *ies*; as, Day, days.

4. Nouns in *f*, or *fe*, change *f*, or *fe*, into *ves* in the plural; as, Loaf, loaves; life, lives.

OBSERVATIONS.

Nouns ending in *ch*, sounding *k*, form the plural by adding *s* only; as, Stomach, stomachs.

Nouns in *o*, with junto, canto, tyro, grotto, portico, solo, and quarto, have *s* only in the plural; as, Folio, folios; canto, cantos.

Nouns in *ff* have their plural in *s*; as, Muff, muffs; except staff, which sometimes has staves.

Dwarf, scarf, wharf; brief, chief, grief, kerchief, handkerchief, mischief; gulf, turf, surf; fife, strife; proof, hoof, roof, and reproof, never change *f* or *fe*, into *ves*—14 change *f* or *fe*, into *ves*, 27 don't—K. p. 22, b

Nouns are either *proper* or *common*.—*Proper* nouns are the names of persons, places, seas, and rivers, &c.; as, *Thomas, Scotland, Forth.*

Common nouns are the names of things in general; as, *Chair, table.*

Collective nouns are nouns that signify many; as, *Multitude, crowd.*

Abstract nouns are the names of qualities abstracted from their substances; as, *Wisdom, wickedness.*

Verbal or *participial* nouns are nouns derived from verbs; as *Reading*

---

* Proper nouns have the plural only when they refer to a race or family; as, The Campbells: or to several persons of the same name as, The eight Henrys; the two Mr. Bells; the two Miss Browns; (or without the numeral) the Miss Roys; but, in addressing letters in which both or all are equally concerned, and also when the names are different, we pluralize the title, (Mr. or Miss) and write Misses Brown: Misses Roy; Messrs. (fo. Messieurs Fr.' Guthrie and Tait

English Etymology.

Exercises on Number.
Write,—or tell,—or spell, the Plural of

Fox,* book, leaf, candle, hat, loaf, wish, fish, sex, kiss, coach, inch, sky, bounty, army, duty, knife, ĕcho, loss, cargo, wife, story, church, table, glass, study, calf, branch, streets, potato, peach, sheaf, booby, rock, stone, house, glory, hope, flower, city, difficulty, distress.

Day, boy, relay, chimney,† journey, valley, needles enemy, an army, a vale, an ant, a sheep, the hills, a valley, the sea, key, toy.

Correct the following errors.

A end, a army, an heart, an horn, an bed, a hour, a adder, a honour, an horse, an house, an pen, a ox, vallies, chimnies, journies, attornies, a eel, a ant, a inch, a eye

Exercises on the Observations.

Monarch, tyro, grotto, nuncio, punctilio, ruff, muff, reproof, portico, handkerchief, gulf, hoof, fife, multitude, people, meeting, John, Lucy, meekness, charity, folly, France, Matthew, James, wisdom, reading.

---

* What is the plural of *fox? Foxes*. Why? Because nouns in *s, sh, ch, x,* or *o,* form the plural by adding *es*.—What is the plural of *book? Books*. Why? Because the plural is generally formed by adding *s* to the singular.—What is the plural of *leaf? Leaves*. Why? Because nouns in *f* or *fe,* change *f* or *fe* into *ves* in the plural.—What is the plural of *army? Armies*. Why? Because nouns in *y* change *y* into *ies* in the plural. What is the plural of *day? Days*. Spell it; *d, a, y, s*. Why not *d, a, i, e, s?* Because *y* with a *vowel* before it is not changed into *ies*:—it takes *s* only.—What is the difference between *adding* and *changing?*—K. No. 37, 40, 41.

† Many eminent authors change *ey* in the singular into *ies* in the plural, thus: *Chimnies* with scorn rejecting smoke *Swift*
    Still as thou dost thy radiant *journies* run. *Prior.*
    But rattling nonsense in full *vallies* breaks. *Pope.*
    The society of Procurators or *Attornies*. *Boswell.*

This mode of spelling these and similar words is highly improper and inconsistent as "*Attornied*." "*Journeyed*."

ENGLISH ETYMOLOGY.

Of Nouns.

Some Nouns are irregular in the formation of their plural: such as—

Singular	Plural.	Singular	Plural.
Man*	men	Tooth	teeth
Woman	women	Goose	geese
Child	children	Mouse	mice
Foot	feet	Louse	lice
Ox	oxen	Penny	pence

* The compounds of man form the plural like the simple; namely, by changing a of the singular into e of the plural.—*Musselman*, not being a compound of man, is *musselmans*, it is said, in the plural; but it should always be musselmen in the plural.

Singular.	Plural.
Brother	brothers, or brethren†
Sow or swine‡	sows, or swine
Die (for gaming)	dice
Die (for coining)	dies
Aide-de-camp	aides-de-camp
Court-martial	courts-martial
Cousin-german	cousins-german
Father-in-law, &c.	fathers-in-law, &c.

† The word *brethren* is generally applied to the members of the same society or church, and *brothers* to the sons of the same parents.

OBSERVATIONS.

Names of *metals, virtues, vices,* and things that are *weighed* or *measured*, &c., are in general singular, as Gold, meekness, drunkenness, bread, beer, beef, &c., except when the different *sorts* are meant, as Wines, teas.

Some nouns are used only in the plural; such as *Antipodes, literati, credenda, minutiæ, banditti, data, folk.*

The singular of *literati*, &c., is made by saying *one of the literati*. *Bandit,* the singular of *banditti,* is often used in newspapers.

The words *Apparatus, hiatus, series, brace, dozen, means,* and *species* are alike in both numbers. Some pluralize *series* into *serieses*. Brace, dozen, &c., sometimes admit of the plural form; thus, He bought partridges in braces, and books in dozens, &c.

News and *alms* are generally used in the singular number, but sometimes in the plural.—*Pains* is generally plural.

‡ The singular of some nouns is distinguished from the plural by the article *a*; as, *A sheep, a swine.*

Pease and *fish* are used when we mean the *species*; as, Pease are dear, fish is cheap; but when we refer to the *number*, we say, Peas, fishes; as, Ten peas; two fishes.

Horse and *foot,* meaning *cavalry* and *infantry,* are used in the singular form with a plural verb; as, A thousand *horse* were ready; ten thousand *foot* were there.—*Men* is understood.

Of Nouns.

As the following words, from Foreign Languages, seldom occur except a few, the pupil may very properly be allowed to omit them, till he be further advanced.

animálculum	animálcula	Fŏcus	fŏcī
Antíthesis	antítheses	Gĕnius	gĕniï†
Apex	apices	Gĕnus	gĕnera
Appendix	{ appendixes, appendices }	Hypŏthesis	hypŏtheses
		Ignis fătuus	ignes fătuī
		Index	indexes, indices‡
Arcânum	arcāna	Lămĭna	lămĭnae
Autŏmaton	autŏmata	Măgus	măgi
Axis*	axes	Memorandum	{ memoranda, or memorandums }
Băsis	băses		
Calx	calces		
Cherub	cherubim, cherubs	Mĕtamorphŏsis	{ mĕtamorphŏses }
Crísis	críses		
Critĕrion	critĕria	Monsieur	messieurs
Dătum	dăta	Phenŏmenon	phenŏmena
Desiderătum	desiderăta	Rădius	rădii
Diaerĕsis	diaerĕses	Stămen	stămĭna
Efflŭvium	efflŭvia	Sĕraph	sĕraphim, sĕraphs
Ellipsis	ellipses	Stĭmulus	stĭmulī
Emphasis	emphases	Stratum	strata
Encŏmium	{ encŏmia, encŏmiums }	Vertex	vĕrtĭces
		Vortex	vŏrtĭces
Errātum	errāta	Virtuŏso	virtuŏsi

¹ It was thought unnecessary to give a list of such words of our own; as, *snuffers, scissors, tongs,* &c., because they are evidently to be used as plural; but it may be proper to observe that such words as *Mathematics, metaphysics, politics, ethics, pneumatics,* &c., though generally *plural,* are sometimes *construed* as *singular,* as, Mathematics *is* a science; and so of the rest.

---

* *Rule.* Nouns in *um* or *on* have *a* in the plural; and those which have *is* in the singular have *es* in the plural.

† *Genii,* aërial spirits; but *geniuses,* persons of genius. For what reason L. *Murray, Elphinston, Oulton,* and others, pluralize such words as *genius* and *rebus,* by adding *ses* to the singular, making them *geniusses, rebusses,* instead of *geniuses, rebuses,* it is not easy to guess; as words ending with a single *s* are never accented on the *last* syllable, there can be no good reason for *doubling* the *s* before *es.* Hence rule 2d, page 7th, begins with "Nouns in *s,*" because those in *ss* include those in *s.*

‡ *Indexes,* when it signifies pointers, or tables of contents *Indices,* when it refers to algebraic quantities.

Of Gender.

Gender is the distinction of sex.

There are three genders; the *Masculine Feminine*, and *Neuter*.

The Masculine denotes the *male* sex; as *A man, a boy*.

The Feminine denotes the *female* sex; as, *A woman, a girl*.

The Neuter denotes whatever is *without life*; as, *Milk*.

There are three ways of distinguishing the sex.

1. By different words; as,

Male	Female.	Male.	Female.
Bachelor	maid, spinster	Horse	mare
Beau	belle	Husband	wife
Boar	sow	King	queen
Boy	girl	Lad	lass
Brother	sister	Lord	lady
Buck	doe	Man	woman
Bull	cow	Master	mistress
Bullock	} heifer,—*hif-er*	Milter	spawner
Ox, or steer		Nephew	niece
Cock	hen	Ram	ewe
Colt	filly	Singer	{ songstress *or* singer
Dog	bitch		
Drake	duck	Sloven	slut
Earl	countess	Son	daughter
Father	mother	Stag	hind
Friar	nun	Uncle	aunt
Gander	goose	Wizard	witch
Hart	roe	Sir	madam

OBSERVATIONS.

Some nouns are either *masculine* or *feminine*: such as *parent, child, cousin, infant, servant, neighbour*, &c.

Some nouns, naturally neuter, are converted into the *masculine or feminine* gender; as, when we say of the sun, *He* is setting; and of the moon, *She* is eclipsed.

Of Nouns.

2. By a difference of termination; as,

Male.	Female.	Male.	Female.
Abbot	abbess	Jew	Jewess
Actor	actress	Landgrave	landgravine
Admĭnistrātor	administrātrix	Lion	lioness
Adulterer	adulteress	Marquis	marchioness
Ambassador	ambassadress	Mayor	mayoress
Arbiter	arbitress	Pātron	pātroness
Author (often)	authoress*	Peer	peeress
Bāron	bāroness	Poet	poetess
Bridegroom	bride	Priest	priestess
Benefactor	benefactress	Prince	princess
Căterer	căteress	Prior	prioress
Chanter	chantress	Prophet	prophetess
Conductor	conductress	Protector	protectress
Count	countess	Shepherd	shepherdess
Deacon	deaconess	Songster	songstress
Duke	duchess	Sorcerer	sorceress
Elector	electress	Sultan	sultaness, or
Emperor	empress		sultāna
Enchanter	enchantress	Tiger	tigress
Exĕcutor	exĕcutrix	Traitor	traitress
Governor	governess	Tutor	tutoress
Heir	heiress	Tyrant	tyranness
Hēro	hĕr-o-īne	Vīscount	vīscountess
Hunter	huntress	Vōtary	vōtaress
Hōst	hōstess	Widower	widow

3. By prefixing another word; as,

A *cock*-sparrow; a *hen*-sparrow; a *he*-goat, a *she*-goat; a *man* servant; a *maid*-servant; a *he*-ass; a *she*-ass, a *male*-child, &c, *male*-descendants, &c.

---

* It does not appear to be necessary, nor even proper, to use *author ess*; for the female noun or pronoun that almost invariably accompanies this word will distinguish the gender in it as well as in *writer*, &c.

Of the CASES of Nouns.

Case is the relation one noun bears to another, or to a verb, or preposition.

Nouns have three cases; the *Nominative, Possessive,* and *Objective.**

The Nominative and Objective are *alike.*

The Possessive is formed by adding an *apostrophe* and *s* to the Nominative; as, *Jōb's.*

When the plural ends in *s,* the possessive is formed by adding only an *apostrophe:* thus,—

Singular.	Plural.	Singular.	Plural.
Nom. Lady	Ladies.	John	——†
Poss. Lady's	Ladies'	John's	——
Obj. Lady	Ladies.	John	——

* *Proper names generally want the plural.*—See p. 7th, last note

EXERCISES.

On Gender, Number, and Case.

‡ Father, brothers, mother's, boys, book, loaf, arms, wife, hats, sisters', bride's, bottles, brush, goose, eagles' wings, echo, ox's horn, mouse, kings, queens, bread, child's, glass, tooth, tongs, candle, chair, Jane's boots, Robert's shoe, horse.

---

* The *Nominative* merely denotes the *name* of a thing.

The *Possessive* denotes *possession;* as, *Ann's* book.—Possession is often expressed by *of* as well as by an '*s*—K. 57 to 63. also 194 and 195

The *Objective* denotes the *object* upon which an active verb or preposition terminates.

‡ One method of using the above exercises is as follows:—

Father, a noun, *singular* (number,) *masculine* (gender,) the *nominative* (case,) plural, fathers. Brothers, a noun, *plural, masculine,* the *nominative.* Mother's, a noun, *singular, feminine,* the *possessive.*—Spell it.—K. 44.

By parsing in this manner, the pupil gives a correct answer to the questions: What part of speech is *father?* What *number?* What *gender?* What *case?* without obliging the teacher *to lose time* to no purpose in asking them.—The pupil, however, should be made to understand that he is giving *answers* to questions which are always supposed to be asked.

As the Nominative and Objective are alike, no inaccuracy can result from the pupil's being allowed to call it always the nominative, till he come to the verb.—*Case* may be altogether *omitted* till that time the cases of pronouns excepted. *See Notes,* p. 30

Of Adjectives.

An *Adjective* is a word which expresses the *quality* of a noun; as, A *good* boy.

Adjectives have *three* degrees of comparison the *Positive, Comparative,* and *Superlative.*

The comparative is formed by adding *er* to the positive; and the superlative by adding *est*; as, *Sweet, sweeter, sweetest.*—K. 67.

Dissyllables in *y* change *y* into *i* before *er* and *est*; as in *Happy, happier, happiest.*†

ADJECTIVES COMPARED IRREGULARLY

Positive.	Comparative.	Superlative
Good, (well an *Adv.*)	better	best
Bad, evil, or ill	worse	worst
Little	less	least
Much or many	more	most
Late	later	latest or last
Near	nearer	nearest or next
Far	farther	farthest
Fore	former	foremost or first
Old	older or elder	oldest or eldest

OBSERVATIONS.

* The *Positive* expresses the *simple* quality; the *Comparative* a *higher* or *lower* degree of the quality; and the Superlative the *highest* or *lowest* degree.—K. 68, 72.

Adjectives of one syllable are generally compared by adding *er* and *est*; and those of more than one, by prefixing *more* and *most*; as *More* numerous, *most* numerous, or, by *less* and *least*; as, *Less* merry, *least* merry.

Dissyllables ending with *e* final are often compared by *e* r and *est*; as, *Polite, politer, politest; Ample, ampler, amplest.*

† If a vowel precede *y*, it is not changed into *i*, before *er* and *est* as, *Gay, gayer, gayest; Coy, coyer, coyest.*

Some Adjectives are compared by adding *most* to the end of the word; as, *Upper, uppermost.*—Some have no positive; as, *Exterior extreme.*

Nouns are often used as *Adjectives;* as, A *gold*-ring, a *silver*-cup *Adjectives* often become Nouns; as, Much *good.*

Some Adjectives do not properly admit of comparison; such as, *True, perfect, universal, chief, extreme,* &c.

Much is applied to things *weighed* or *measured; Many* to those that are *numbered*—*Elder* and *eldest* to persons; *older* and *eldest* to things.

When the positive ends in a single consonant, preceded by a single vowel, the consonant is doubled before *er* and *est;* as, *Big, bigger, biggest.*

Of Personal Pronouns.

A *Pronoun* is a word used instead of a noun; as, *John* is a good boy; *he* obeys the master

There are three kinds of pronouns; Personal, Relative, and Adjective.—The Personal Pronouns are thus declined:—

	Singular.			Plural.		
	Nom.	Poss.	Obj.	Nom.	Poss.	Obj.
First Personal Pronoun m. or f.	I	mine	me	We	ours	us
2. m. or f.	Thou	thine	thee	You*	yours	you
3. m.	He	his	him	}		
3. f.	She	hers†	her	} They	theirs	them.
3. n.	It	its	it	}		

Exercises on Personal Pronouns.

I, thou, we, me, us, thine, he, him, she hers, they, thee, them, its, theirs, you, her ours, yours, mine, his, I, me, them, us, it, we

---

* *Ye* is often used instead of *you* in the nominative: as, *Ye* are happy.

Mine and *thine* were *formerly* used instead of *my* and *thy* before a vowel or an *h*; as, Blot out all *mine* iniquities; Give me *thine* heart

† *Hers, its, ours, yours, theirs,* should never be written, *her's, its, our's, your's, their's*; but *hers, its, ours, &c.*

The compound personal pronouns, *Myself, thyself, himself, &c.* are commonly joined either to the simple pronoun, or to any ordinary noun to make it more remarkable.—See K. 80, 96.

These pronouns are all generally in the *same case* with the noun or pronoun to which they are joined; as, "*She herself* said so;" "*They themselves* acknowledged it to *me myself.*" "The master *himself* got it."

Self, when used alone, is a noun, as, "Our fondness for *self* is a evil to others."—K. 96.

In some respectable Grammars the possessive case of the different personal pronouns stands thus: 1st, *my* or *mine, our* or *ours*—2d, *thy* or *thine, your* or *yours*—3d, *her* or *hers, their* or *theirs*. I see no impropriety in this method; the one I have preferred, however, is perhaps less liable to objection

Of Relative Pronouns.

A *Relative* Pronoun is a word that relates to a noun or pronoun before it, called the antecedent; as, The master who taught us, &c.*

The simple relatives are *who, which,* and *that;* they are alike in both numbers, thus,

Nom. Who.
Poss. Whose.
Obj. Whom

Who is applied to persons; as, The boy *who.*†

Which is applied to inferior *animals,* and things without life; as, The dog *which* barks, the book *which* was lost.

That is often used instead of *who* or *which*, as, The boy *that* reads; the book *that* was lost.

What is a compound relative, including both the relative and the antecedent;‡ as, This is *what* I wanted; that is, *the thing which* I wanted.

OBSERVATIONS.

In asking questions, *Who, which,* and *what,* are called *Interrogatives*; as, *Who* said that? *What* did he do?—K. p. 84, *Note.*

The relative is always of the *same gender, number,* and *person* with its antecedent, but not always in the same *case.*—K. p. 43,† *b.*

Which has properly no possessive case of its own. The objective with *of* before it supplies its place. Our best writers, however, now use *whose* as the possessive of *which;* as, "A religion *whose* origin is divine." BLAIR. See more remarks on *Which,* at p. 151.—For the relative *as,* see p. 146.

* The relative sometimes refers to a *whole clause* as its antecedent: as, The Bill was rejected by the Lords, which excited no small degree of jealousy and discontent; that is, which *thing* or *circumstance, excited, &c.*

† *Who* is applied to inferior animals, when they are represented as speaking and acting like *rational beings.*—K. p. 43,* *b.*

‡ *What* and *which* are sometimes used as *adjectives*, as, "I know not by *what* fatality the adversaries of the motion are impelled;" *which* things are an allegory. *Which* here is equal to *these.*—P. 67. *b*

Whoever, whosoever, and *whoso,* are compound relatives equal to *He who;* or, *The person that.*—K. 88.

Whatever and *whatsoever,* with *whichever* and *whichsoever,* are sometimes adjectives, and combine with nouns, and sometimes compound

ADJECTIVE PRONOUNS

There are four sorts of Adjective Pronouns.

1. The Possessive Pronouns, *My, thy, his,*[*] *her, our, your, their, its, own.*[†]

2. The Distributive, *Each, every, either, either.*

3. The Demonstrative, *This, that,*[‡] with their plurals, *these, those.*[§]

4. The Indefinite, *None, any, all, such, whole, some, both, one, other, another :* the last three are declined like nouns.

OBSERVATIONS.

relatives, equal to *that which.* These compounds, however, particularly *whoso,* are now generally avoided. *Whatever* and *whoever* are most used.

[*] *His* and *her* are possessive pronouns when placed immediately before nouns; but when they stand by themselves, *his* is accounted the possessive case of the *personal* pronoun *he,* and *her* the objective of *she.*

[†] *Its* and *own* seem to be as much entitled to the appellation of possessive pronouns as *his* and *my.*

[‡] *Yon.* with *former* and *latter,* may be called demonstrative pronouns, as well as *this* and *that.* See Syntax, R. 28, b.

[§] *That* is sometimes a *Relative,* sometimes a *Demonstrative* pronoun, and sometimes a *Conjunction.*—K. 90.

That is a *Relative* when it can be turned into *who* or *which,* without destroying the sense; as, "The days *that* (or which) are past are gone for ever."

That is a *Demonstrative* pronoun when it is placed immediately before a noun, expressed or understood; as, "*That* book is new." "*That* is not the one I want."

That is a *Conjunction* when it cannot be turned into *who* or *which,* but marks a consequence, an indication, or final end: as, "He was so proud *that* he was universally despised." He answered, "*That* he never was so happy as he is now." Live well, *that* you may die well.

All the *indefinite* pronouns, (except *none,*) and even the *demonstrative, distributive,* and *possessive,* are *adjectives* belonging to nouns either expressed or understood; and in parsing I think they ought to be called adjectives.—*None* is used in *both* numbers; but it cannot be joined to a noun.

The phrase *none other* should be *no other.*—*Another* has no plural.

Promiscuous exercises on NOUNS, &c.

A man, he, who, which, that, his, me, mine thine, whose, they, hers, it, we, us, I, him, its, horse, mare, master, thou, theirs, thee, you, my, thy, our, your, their, his, her—this, these, that, those—each, every, either, any, none, bride, daughter, uncle, wife's, sir. girl, madam, box, dog, lad, a gay lady; sweet apples; strong bulls; fat oxen; a mountainous country.

Compare, Rich, merry, furious, covetous, large, little, good, bad, near, wretched, rigorous, delightful, sprightly, spacious, splendid, gay, imprudent, pretty.

The human mind; cold water; he, thou, she, it; woody mountains; the naked rock; youthful jollity; goodness divine; justice severe; his, thy, others, one, a peevish boy hers, their strokes; pretty girls; his droning flight; her delicate cheeks; a man who; the sun that; a bird which; its pebbled bed; fiery darts; a numerous army; love unbounded, a nobler victory; gentler gales; nature's eldest birth; earth's lowest room; the winds triumphant; some flowery stream; the tempestuous billows; these things; those books that breast which; the rich man's insolence your queen; all who; a boy's drum; himself, themselves, myself.*

---

* The personal pronouns, *Himself, herself, themselves*, &c., are used in the *nominative* case as well as in the objective; as, *Himself* shall come.

Mr. Blair, in his Grammar, says, they have only one case, viz, the *nominative*, but this is a mistake, for they have the *objective* too.—E. &c.

ENGLISH ETYMOLOGY

Of VERBS.

A verb is a word that *affirms* something of its nominative; or,

A *Verb* is a word which expresses *being, doing or suffering*; as, I *am*,—I *love*,—I *am loved*.

Verbs are of three kinds, *Active, Passive,* and *Neuter*.

A verb *Active* expresses action passing from an *actor* to an *object*; as, James *strikes* the table.*

A verb *Passive* expresses the suffering of an action, or the *enduring* of what *another* does; as, The table *is struck*.

A verb *Neuter* expresses *being*, or a *state* of *being*, or action confined to the *actor*; as, I *am*, he *sleeps*, you *run*.†

AUXILIARY VERBS.

The auxiliary or helping verbs, by which verbs are chiefly inflected, are defective, having only the Present and Past Indicative; thus,

Pres. Do, have, shall, will, may, can, am, must.
Past. Did, had, should, would, might, could, was, must.

And the Participles (of *be*) *being, been*—*Be, do have,* and *will*, are often *principal* verbs.‡

Let is an *active* verb, and complete. *Ought* is a *defective* verb. having only the *Present* and *Past* Indicative.—P. 47, mid.

---

* *Active* verbs are called *transitive* verbs, because the action passes from the actor to the object.—K. p. 58, Note.

† *Neuter* verbs are called *intransitive*, because their action is confined to the actor, and does not pass over to an object.—*Children should not be troubled too soon with the distinction between active and neuter verbs.*

‡ It was thought quite unnecessary to conjugate the verbs *have* and *do*, &c., through all their moods and tenses; because a child that can easily conjugate the verb to *love*, can easily conjugate any other verb.

A verb is declined by Voices Moods, Tenses, Numbers, and Persons.

Of the Moods of Verbs.

Verbs have *five* moods; namely, the Indicative, Potential, Subjunctive, Imperative, and Infinitive.

The *Indicative* mood simply declares a thing; as, He *loves;* he is *loved;* or it asks a question; as, *Lovest* thou me?

The *Potential* mood implies possibility liberty, power, will, or obligation; as, The wind *may* blow; we *may* walk or ride; I *can* swim; he *would* not stay; you *should* obey your parents.

The *Subjunctive* mood represents a thing under a condition, supposition, motive, wish, &c., and is preceded by a conjunction expressed or understood, and followed by another verb; as, If thy presence *go* not with us, *carry* us not up hence.

The *Imperative* mood commands, exhorts, entreats, or permits; as, *Do* this; *remember* thy Creator; *hear,* O my people; *go* thy way.

The *Infinitive* mood expresses a thing in a general manner, without distinction of number or person, and commonly has *to* before it; as, *To love.*

Explanations of the moods and tenses of verbs are inserted here for the sake of order; but it would be highly improper to detain the learner so long as to commit them to memory; he ought, therefore, after getting the definition of a verb, to proceed to the inflection of it without delay; and, when he comes to the exercises on the verbs, he can look back to the definition of a verb active, &c., as occasion may require.

Of Tenses, or Distinctions of Time.

The *Present tense* expresses what is going on just now; as, I *love* you; I *strike* the table.

The *Past tense* represents the action or event either as past and finished; as, He *broke* the bottle and *spilt* the brandy; or it represents the action as unfinished at a certain time past; as, My father *was coming* home when I met him.

The *Perfect tense* implies that an action has just now, or lately, been quite finished; as, John *has cut* his finger; I *have sold* my horse.

The *Pluperfect tense* represents a thing as *past*, before another event happened; as, All the judges *had taken* their places, *before* Sir Roger came.

The *Future* represents the action as yet to come; as, I *will see* you again, and your heart *shall rejoice*.*

The *Future Perfect* intimates that the action will be fully accomplished, at, or before the time of another future action or event; as, I *shall have* got my lesson *before* ten o'clock to morrow.

---

* Mr Walker and others have divided the first future into the *future foretelling*, and the *future promising* or *commanding*. That this distinction is absolutely necessary, as Mr. Walker affirms, is exceedingly questionable; for when a learner has occasion to use the future tense, this division will not in the least assist him in determining whether he ought to use *will* rather than *shall*, &c Therefore this division serves no purpose

Remarks on some of the Tenses.

ON THE PRESENT

1. The *Present Tense* is used to express a *habit* or *custom* as, He *snuffs*; She *goes* to church. It is sometimes applied to persons long since dead, when the narration of their actions excites our passions, as, "Nero *is* abhorred for his cruelty." "Milton *is* admired for his sublimity."

2. In historical narration it is beautifully used for the *Past Tense* as, "Cesar *leaves* Gaul *crosses* the Rubicon, and *enters* Italy with five thousand men." It is sometimes used with fine effect for the Perfect; as, "In the Book of Genesis, Moses *tells* us who were the descendants of Abraham,"—for *has told* us.

3. When preceded by such words as *when, before, as soon as, after*, it expresses the relative time of a *future* action; as, When he *comes*, he will be welcome—As soon as the post *arrives*, the letters will be delivered.

4. In the *continuate, progressive*, or *compound form*, it expresses an action *begun* and *going on just now*, but not complete; as, I *am studying* my lesson. He *is writing* a letter.

ON THE PAST

The *Past Tense* is used when the action or state is *limited* by the *circumstance* of *time* or *place:* as, "We *saw* him *yesterday*." "We were in bed *when he arrived*." Here the words *yesterday* and *when* limit the action and state to a particular time —After *death* all agents are spoken of in the *Past Tense*, because time is limited or defined by the *life* of the person; as, "Mary Queen of Scots *was* remarkable for her beauty."

This tense is peculiarly appropriated to the *narrative style;* because all narration implies some *circumstance;* as, "Socrates *refused* to adore false gods." Here the period of Socrates' life, being a limited part of past time, circumscribes the narration. It is improper then to say of one already dead, "He *has been* much admired; he *has done* much good:" but, "He *was* much admired; he *did* much good."

Although the Past Tense is used when the action is *circumstantially* expressed by a word or sentiment that limits the time of the action to some definite portion of past time, yet such words as *often, sometimes, many a time, frequently*, and similar vague intimations of time, except in *narrations*, require the *perfect*, because they admit a certain latitude, and do not limit the action to any definite portion of past time—thus, "How *often have we seen* the proud despised."

ON THE PERFECT.

The *Perfect Tense* chiefly denotes the accomplishment of mere acts, without any *necessary* relation to *time* or *place*, or any other circumstance of their existence; as, Philosophers *have endeavoured* to investigate the origin of evil. In general, however, it denotes,

1. An action newly finished; as, I *have heard* great news. The post *has arrived*, but he *has brought* no letters for you.

2. An action done in a *definite* space of time, (such as a *day*, a *week*, a *year*,) a part of which has yet to *elapse*; as, I *have spent* this day well.

3. An action perfected some time ago, but whose consequences extend to the present time, as, We *have neglected* our duty, and are therefore unhappy.

Duration or *existence* requires the *perfect*; as, He *has been* dead four days. We say, Cicero *has written* orations, because the orations are still in *existence*; but we cannot say, Cicero *has written* poems, because the poems do not exist; they are lost; therefore, we must say, "Cicero *wrote* poems."

The following are a few instances in which this tense is improperly used for the past. "I have somewhere met with the epitaph of a charitable man, which *has* very much *pleased* me." Spect. No. 177. The latter part of this sentence is rather *narrative* than *assertive:* and therefore it should be—which very much *pleased* me, that is, *when I read* it.—" When that the poor *hath* cried, Cesar *hath* wept." Shakesp. The style is here *narrative:* Cesar was dead. It should therefore be, "When the poor *cried*, Cesar *wept*.—"Though in old age, the circle of our pleasures is more contracted than it *has formerly been;* yet," &c. Blair, Sermon 12. It should be, "than it formerly *was;*" because in old age, the former stages of life contrasted with the present, convey an idea, not of *completion*, but of *limitation*, and thus become a subject of *narration*, rather than of *assertion*.—"I have known him, Eugenius, *when he has been* going to a play, or an opera, divert the money which was designed for that purpose upon an object of charity whom he *has met with* in the street." Spect. No. 177. It should be, "when he *was going*," and "whom he *met* with in the street;" because the actions are *circumstantially* related by the phrases, *when going to a play*, and *in the street*.

ON THE FUTURE PERFECT.

Upon more careful reflection, it appears to me, that the second future should have *will* or *shall* in *all* the persons, as in the *first* *tr.* Murray has excluded *will* from the *first* person, and *shall* from the *second* and *third*, because they appear to him to be incorrectly applied; and in the examples which he has adduced, they are incorrectly applied; but this is not a sufficient reason for excluding them altogether from every sentence. The fault is in the writer; he has applied them wrong, a thing that is often done with *will* and *shall* in the *first* future, as well as in the second.

If I am at liberty to use *will* in the *first* future, to intimate my *resolution* to perform a future action, as, I *will* go to church, for am *resolved* to go," why should I not employ *will* in the *second* future, to intimate my resolution or determination to have a action *finished* before a specified future time? Thus, "I *will* have written my letters before supper:" that is, I am *determined* to have my letters finished before supper. Were the truth of this affirmation respecting the time of finishing the letters called in question the propriety of using *will* in the *first* person would be unquestionable. Thus, You will not have finished your letters before supper, I am sure. Yes, *I will*—Will what? "Will have finished my letters."

Shall, in like manner, may with propriety be applied to the *second* and *third* person. In the *third* person, for instance, if I say, "He *will* have paid me his bill before June," I merely foretell what he will have done; but that is not what I intended to say. I meant to convey the idea, that since I have found him so dilatory, I will compel him to pay it before June; and as this was my meaning, I *should* have employed *shall*, as in the first future, and said, "He *shall* have paid me his bill before June."

It is true that we seldom use this future : we rather express the idea as nearly as we can by the *first* future, and say, "He shall pay his bill before June;" but when we do use the *second* future, it is evident, I trust, from the examples just given, that *shall* and *will* should be applied in it exactly as they are in the *first*.—*See* 1 Cor xv. 24.—*Luke* xvii. 10.

On the Auxiliary Verbs.

The auxiliary verbs, as they are called, such as, *Do, shall, will, may, can*, and *must*, are in reality *separate* verbs, and were originally used as such, having after them, either the Past Participle, or the *Infinitive* Mood, with the *to* suppressed, for the sake of sound, as it is after *bid, dare*, &c. (See Syntax, Rule VI.) Thus, I *have loved* We *may to* love. He *will to* speak. I *do to* write. I *may to* have loved. We *might to* have got a prize. I *would to* have given him the book. All *must to* die. I *shall to* stop. I *can to* go.

These verbs are always joined in this manner either to the *Infinitive* or participle, and although this would be a simpler way of parsing the verb than the common, yet in compliment, perhaps, to the

Greek and Latin, grammarians in general consider the auxiliary and the following verb in the infinitive or participle as *one* verb, and parse and construe it accordingly.

Several of the auxiliaries in the Potential Mood refer to *present*, *past*, and *future* time. This needs not excite surprise; for even the Present Indicative can be made to express *future* time, as well as the future itself. Thus, "He *leaves* town *to-morrow*."

Present time is expressed in the following sentence: "I wish he *could* or *would* come just now."

Past time is expressed with the similar auxiliaries; as, "It *was* my desire that he *should* or *would* come yesterday." "Though he *was* ill he *might* recover."

Future.—I am anxious that he *should*, or *would* come to-morrow. If he come, I *may* speak to him. If he would delay his journey a few days, I *might*, *could*, *would*, or *should* accompany him.

Although such examples as these are commonly adduced as proofs that these auxiliaries refer to *present*, *past*, and *future* time, yet I think it is pretty evident that *might*, *could*, *would*, and *should*, with *may*, and *can*, merely express *liberty*, *ability*, *will*, and *duty*, without any reference to time at all, and that the precise time is generally determined by the drift or scope of the sentence, or rather by the *adverb* or participle that is subjoined or understood, and not by these auxiliaries.

Must or *ought*, for instance, merely imply *necessity* and *obligation*, without any necessary relation to *time*; for when I say, "I must do it," *must* merely denotes the *necessity* I am under, and *do* the present time, which might easily be made *future*, by saying, "I must do it *next week:*" Here future time is expressed by *next week*, and not by *must*. If I say, "I must have done it:" Here *must* merely expresses *necessity*, as before, and I *have done* the *past time*. "These *ought* ye to do:" Here *ought* merely denotes obligation, and *do* the *present* time. "These ought ye to have done:" Here *ought* merely expresses *duty* or *obligation*, as before; but the time of its existence is denoted as past, by to *have done*, and not by *ought*, as Mr. Murray and many others say.

As *must* will not admit of the *objective* after it, nor is even preceded or succeeded by the *sign* of the *infinitive*, it has been considered an absolute auxiliary, like *may* or *can*, belonging to the Potential Mood.

Ought, on the contrary, is an independent verb, though defective and always governs another verb in the infinitive.

Of Will and Shall.

Will, in the *first* person singular and *plural*, intimates *resolution* and *promising*; as, I *will* not let thee go, except thou bless me We *will* go. I *will* make of thee a great nation.

Will, in the *second* and *third* person,[*] commonly *foretells*; as, He *will* reward the righteous. You, or they, *will* be very happy there.

Shall, in the *first* person, only *foretells*; as, I, or we *shall* go to-morrow. In the *second* and *third* person, *Shall*, *promises*, *commands*, or *threatens*; as, They, or you, *shall* be rewarded. Thou *shalt* not steal. The soul that sinneth *shall* die.

But this must be understood of affirmative sentences only; so when the sentence is interrogative, just the reverse commonly takes place; as, *Shall* I send you a little of the pie? i. e. *will you permit* me to send it? *Will* James return to-morrow? i. e. do you expect him?

When the *second* and *third person*[*] are represented as the subjects of their own expressions, or their own thoughts, SHALL foretells, as in the *first* person; as, "He says he *shall* be a loser by this bargain." "Do you suppose you *shall* go?" and WILL promises, as in the first person; as, "He says he *will* bring Pope's Homer to-morrow." You say you *will* certainly come.

Of *shall* it may be remarked, that it never expresses the *will* or *resolution* of its *Nominative*: Thus, I *shall* fall; *Thou shalt* love thy neighbour, He *shall* be rewarded—express no resolution on the part of *I, thou, he*.

Did *will*, on the contrary, always intimate the resolution of its *Nominative*, the difficulty of applying *will* and *shall* would be at an end; but this cannot be said; for though *will* in the *first* person always expresses the resolution of its *Nominative*, yet, in the *second* and *third* person, it does not *always foretell*, but often intimates the resolution of its *Nominative* as strongly as it does in the *first* person, thus, Ye *will* not come unto me that ye may have life. He *will* not perform the duty of my husband's brother, *Deut*. xxv. 7; see also verse 9. Accordingly *would*, the past time of *will*, is used in the same manner; as, And he was angry, and *would* not go in, *Luke* xv. 28.

Should and *would* are subject to the same rules as *shall* and *will*; they are generally attended with a supposition; as, Were I to run, I *should* soon be fatigued, &c.

Should is often used instead of *ought*, to express duty or obligation; as, We *should* remember the poor. We *ought* to obey God rather than men.

---

[*] See Page 141. Obs 3d.

Of Verbs.

To Love   *Active Voice*

Indicative Mood.
Present Tense.

Singular.	*Plural.*
person 1. I love	1. We love
2. Thou lovest	2. You* love
3. He loves or loveth	3. They love

Past Tense.

Singular.	*Plural.*
1. I loved	1. We loved
2. Thou lovedst	2. You loved
3. He loved	3. They love

Perfect Tense.
Its signs are, *have, hast, has, or hath.*

Singular.	*Plural.*
1. I have loved	1. We have loved
2. Thou hast loved	2. You have loved
3. He has or hath loved	3. They have loved

Pluperfect Tense.
Signs, *had, hadst.*

Singular.	*Plural.*
1. I had loved	1. We had loved
2. Thou hadst loved	2. You had loved
3. He had loved	3. They had loved

Future Tense.
Signs, *shall or will.*

Singular.	*Plural.*
1. I shall or will love	1. We shall or will love
2. Thou shalt or wilt love	2. You shall or will love
3. He shall or will love	3. They shall or will love

---

* *You* has always a *plural* verb, even when applied to a *single individual.*

Future Perfect.

[See pages 23, 24.]

Singular.	Plural.
1. Shall *or* will have loved	1. Shall *or* will have loved
2. Shalt *or* wilt have loved	2. Shall *or* will have loved
3. Shall *or* will have loved	3. Shall *or* will have loved

Potential Mood.

Present.

Signs, *may, can,* or *must.*

Singular.	Plural.
1. May *or* can* love	1. May *or* can love
2. Mayst *or* canst love	2. May *or* can love
3. May *or* can love	3. May *or* can love

Past.

Signs, *might, could, would,* or *should*

Singular.	Plural.
1 Might, could, would, *or* should love	1. Might, could, would, *or* should love
2 Mightst, couldst, wouldst, *or* shouldst love	2. Might, could, would, *or* should love
3 Might, could, would, *or* should love	3 Might, could, would, *or* should love

Perfect.

Signs, *may, can,* or *must have.*

Singular.	Plural.
1. May *or* can* have loved	1. May *or* can have loved
2. Mayst *or* canst have loved	2. May *or* can have loved
3. May *or* can have loved	3. May *or* can have loved

---

* *Must,* although it belongs as properly to the *present* and *perfect* potential as *may* or *can,* has been omitted for want of room; but in going over these tenses, with the auxiliaries, one by one, it is easy to take it in thus: I *must love,* Thou *must love,* &c.—See 2d note, p. 37.

Pluperfect.

Signs, *might, could, would,* or *should have*

Singular.
1 Might, could, would, *or* should have loved
2. Mightst, &c., have loved
3 Might have loved

Plural.
1. Might, could, would, *or* should have loved
2 Might have loved
3. Might have loved

Subjunctive Mood.

Present Tense.

Singular
1. If I love
2. If thou love
3 If he love

Plural.
1. If we love
2. If you love
3. If they love*

Imperative Mood.

Singular.
2 Love, *or* love thou, *or* do thou love†

Plural.
2 Love. *or* love ye, *or* you, *or* do ye love

Infinitive Mood.

Present, To love   *Perfect*, To have loved

PARTICIPLES.

Present, Loving.   *Past*, Loved.   *Perfect*, Having loved.‡

---

* "The remaining tenses of the subjunctive mood are, in every espect, similar to the corresponding tenses of the indicative mood, with the addition to the verb of a conjunction expressed or implied, denoting a condition, motive, wish, or supposition."—See p. 33, note 2d.

† The imperative mood is not entitled to *three* persons. In strict propriety, it has only the *second* person in both numbers. For when say, Let me love: I mean, Permit thou me to love. Hence, *let me love*, is construed thus: *let thou me (to) love*, or do thou *let me to) love*. *To*, the sign of the infinitive, is not used after *let*. See Syntax, R. VI. No one will say that *permit (me* to love) is the *first* person singular, imperative mood: then, why should *let (me* to love,) which is exactly similar, be called the *first* person? The *Latin* verb wants the *first* person, and if it has the *third*, it has also a different termination for it, which is not the case in the English verb —R 118 ——— ‡ See Key, No. 208–211.

Of Verbs.

Exercises on the Tenses of Verbs, and Cases of Nouns and Pronouns.

* We love him; James loves me; it amuses him; we shall conduct them; they will divide the spoil; soldiers should defend their country; friends invite friends; she can read her lesson; she may play a tune; you might please her; thou mayest ask him; he may have betrayed us; we might have diverted the children; John can deliver the message.

I love; to love; love, reprove thou; has loved; we tied the knot; if we love; if thou love; they could have commanded armies; to love; to baptize; to have loved; loved; loving; to survey; having surveyed; write a letter, read your lesson; thou hast obeyed my voice; honour thy father.

The teacher, if he chooses, may now acquaint the learner with the difference between the Nominative and the Objective.

The Nominative *acts;* the Objective is *acted upon;* as, *He* eats *apples.*

The Nominative commonly comes *before* the verb, the Objective after it.

Concerning pronouns, it may be observed, that the first *speaks;* the second is spoken *to;* and the third (or any noun) is spoken *of.*

* We may parse the first sentence, for example. *We love him; We,* the first personal pronoun, plural, masculine or feminine, the Nominative: *love,* a verb active, the first person, plural, present, Indicative; *him,* the third personal pronoun, singular, masculine, the Objective.

QUESTIONS which should be put to the pupils.

How do you know that *love* is plural? *Ans.* Because *we* its Nominative is plural. How do you know that *love* is the first person? *Ans.* Because *we* is the first personal pronoun, and the verb is always of the same number and person with the noun or pronoun before it.—K. 102, 104.

Many of the phrases in this page may be converted into exercises of a different kind; thus the meaning of the sentence, *We love him,* may be expressed by the passive voice; as, *He is loved by us.*

It may also be turned into a question, or made a negative; as, *Do we love him?* &c. *We do not love him.*

These are a few of the ways of using the exercises on a single page; but the variety of methods that every ingenious and diligent teacher may invent and adopt to engage the attention and improve the understanding of his pupils is past finding out

Of Verbs.

TO BE.

Indicative Mood.

Present Tense.

Singular.
1. I am*
2. Thou art
3. He is

Plural.
1. We are
2. You are
3. They are

Past Tense.

Singular.
1. I was
2. Thou wast
3. He was

Plural.
1. We were
2. You were
3. They were

Perfect Tense.

Singular.
1. I have been
2. Thou hast been
3. He has been

Plural.
1. We have been
2. You have been
3. They have been

Pluperfect Tense.

Singular.
1. I had been
2. Thou hadst been
3. He had been

Plural.
1. We had been
2. You had been
3. They had been

Future Tense.

Singular.
1. I shall *or* will be
2. Thou shalt *or* wilt be
3. He shall *or* will be

Plural.
1. We shall *or* will be
2. You shall *or* will be
3. They shall *or* will be

---

* Put *loving* after *am,* &c., and you make it an *Active* verb in the *progressive* form.—Thus, I am *loving,* thou art *loving,* he is *loving,* &c.—P. 39

Put *loved* after *am,* and you will make it a *Passive* verb.—See p 3a.

Of Verbs.

Future Perfect Tense.

Singular.	Plural.
1 Shall or will have been	1. Shall or will have been
2. Shalt or wilt have been	2. Shall or will have been
3. Shall or will have been	3. Shall or will have been

Potential Mood.

Present Tense.

Singular.	Plural.
1 May,* or can be	1. May, or can be
2. Mayst, or canst be	2. May, or can be
3. May, or can be	3. May, or can be

Past.

Singular.	Plural.
1. Might, &c., be	1. Might be
2. Mightst be	2. Might be
3. Might be	3. Might be

Perfect.

Singular.	Plural.
1. May, or can have been	1. May, or can have been
2. Mayst, or canst have been	2. May, or can have been
3 May, or can have been	3. May, or can have been

Pluperfect

Singular.	Plural.
1. Might have been	1. Might have been
2. Mightst have been	2. Might have been
3. Might have been	3. Might have been

---

* See Note, p. 23; also Note 2d, p. 27.

Of Verbs.

Subjunctive Mood.

Present Tense.

Singular.	Plural.
1. If I be*	1. If we be
2. If thou be	2. If you be
3. If he be	3. If they be

Past Tense.

Singular.	Plural.
1. If I were	1. If we were
2. If thou wert	2. If you were
3. If he were	3. If they were†

Imperative Mood.

Singular	Plural.
1. Be, *or* be thou	2. Be, *or* be ye *or* you

Infinitive Mood.

Present, To be *Perfect*, To have been

PARTICIPLES.

Present, Being *Past*, Been *Perfect*, Having been

---

* *Be* is often used in the Scriptures and some other books for the *Present Indicative*; as, We *be* true men, for we *are*.

† The remaining tenses of this mood are, in every respect, similar to the correspondent tenses of the Indicative Mood. But some say, that the Future Perfect, when used with a *conjunction*, has *shall* in *all* the persons: thus, If I *shall* have loved, If thou *shalt* have loved, If he *shall* have loved, If we, you, or they *shall* have loved.— See p 29, note 1st.

Though, unless, except, whether, &c., may be joined to the Subjunctive Mood, as well as *if*

C

Of Verbs.

Exercises on the Verb To Be.

Am, is, art, wast, are, I was, they were we are, hast been, has been, we have been, hadst been, he had been, you have been, she has been, we were, they had been.

I shall be, shalt be, we will be, thou wilt be, they shall be, it will be, thou wilt have been, we have been, they will have been, we shall have been, am, it is.

I can be, mayst be, canst be, she may be, you may be, he must be, they should be, mightst be, he would be, it could be, wouldst be, you could be, he may have been, wast.

We may have been, mayst have been, they can have been, I might have been, you should have been, wouldst have been, (if thou be, we be, he be, thou wert, we were, I be.

Be thou, be, to be, being, to have been, if I be, be ye, been, be, having been, if we be, if they be, to be.

Snow is white; he was a good man; we have been younger; she has been happy; it had been late; we are old; you will be wise; it will be time; if they be thine; be cautious: be heedful youth; we may be rich; they should be virtuous; thou mightst be wiser; they must have been excellent scholars; they might have been powerful.

Of Verbs.

TO BE LOVED.   *Passive Voice.*

Indicative Mood.

Present Tense.

Singular.	Plural
1. Am loved	1. Are loved
2. Art loved	2. Are loved
3. Is loved	3. Are loved

Past Tense.

Singular.	Plural.
1. Was loved	1. Were loved
2. Wast loved	2. Were loved
3. Was loved	3. Were loved

Perfect Tense.

Singular.	Plural.
1. Have been loved	1. Have been loved
2. Hast been loved	2. Have been loved
3. Has been loved	3. Have been loved

Pluperfect Tense.

Singular.	Plural.
1. Had been loved	1. Had been loved
2. Hadst been loved	2. Had been loved
3. Had been loved	3. Had been loved

Future Tense.

Singular.	Plural.
1. Shall *or* will be loved	1. Shall *or* will be loved
2. Shalt *or* wilt be loved	2. Shall *or* will be loved
3. Shall *or* will be loved	3. Shall *or* will be loved

☞ A *Passive* Verb is formed by putting the *Past Participle* of any *active* verb after the verb *to be* through all its moods and tenses.—K. 126, 127

Of Verbs

Future Perfect Tense.

Singular.	Plural.
1. Shall or will have been loved	1. Shall or will have been loved
2. Shalt or will have been loved	2. Shall or will have been loved
3. Shall or will have been loved	3. Shall or will have been loved

Potential Mood.

Present Tense.

Singular.	Plural.
1. May or can be loved	1. May or can be loved
2. Mayst or canst be loved	2. May or can be loved
3. May or can be loved	3. May or can be loved

Past.

Singular.	Plural.
1. Might, &c., be loved	1. Might be loved
2. Mightst be loved	2. Might be loved
3. Might be loved	3. Might be loved

Perfect.

Singular.	Plural
1. May, &c., have been loved	1. May have been loved
2. Mayst have been loved	2. May have been loved
3. May have been loved	3. May have been loved

Pluperfect.

Singular	Plural.
1. Might, &c., have been loved	1. Might have been loved
2. Mightst have been loved	2. Might have been loved
3. Might have been loved	3. Might have been loved

Of Verbs.

Subjunctive Mood.

Present Tense.

Singular.
1. If* I be loved
2. If thou be loved
3. If he be loved

Plural.
1. If we be loved
2. If you be loved
3. If they be loved

Past.

Singular.
1. If I were loved
2. If thou wert loved
3. If he were loved

Plural.
1. If we were loved
2. If you were loved
3. If they were loved

Imperative Mood.

Singular.
2. Be thou loved

Plural.
2. Be ye or you loved

Infinitive Mood.

Present, To be loved   *Perfect,* To have been loved

PARTICIPLES.

Pres. Being loved. *Past.* Been loved *Perf.* Having been loved

---

* The pupil may at times be requested to throw out *if*, and put *unless, though, whether,* or *lest,* in its place.

☞ After the pupil is *expert* in going over the tenses of the verb as they are, he may be taught to omit all the auxiliaries but *one*, and —, over the verb thus   *Present* Potential. I *may* love: thou *mayst* love; he *may* love, &c.; and then with the next auxiliary, thus: I *can* love; thou *canst* love; he *can* love, &c.; and then with *must*, thus: I *must* love; thou *must* love; he *must* love, &c. and then with the auxiliaries of the *Past* Potential, thus: I *might* love, thou *mightst* love &c.

Of Verbs.

Exercises on the Verb Passive

They are loved; we were loved; thou art loved, it is loved; she was loved; he has been loved; you have been loved; I have been loved; thou hadst been loved; we shall be loved; thou wilt be loved; they will be loved; I shall have been loved; you will have been loved.

He can be loved; thou mayst be loved; she must be loved; they might be loved; ye would be loved; they should be loved; I could be loved; thou canst have been loved; it may have been loved; you might have been loved; if I be loved;* thou wert loved, we be loved; they be loved.—Be thou loved; be ye loved; you be loved.—To be loved; loved; having been loved; to have been loved; being loved.

Promiscuous Exercises on Verbs, and Cases of Nouns and Pronouns

Tie John's shoes; this is Jane's bonnet; ask mamma; he has learned his lesson; she invited him; your father may commend you; he was baptized; the minister baptized him; we should have delivered our message; papa will reprove us; divide the apples; the captain had commanded his soldiers to pursue the enemy; Eliza diverted her brother; a hunter killed a hare, were* I loved, were we good we should be happy.†

---

* A conjunction is frequently to be understood here
† See exercises of a different sort, page 52

Of Verbs.

An *Active* or a *Neuter Verb* may be conjugated through all its moods and tenses, by adding its *Present Participle* to the verb *To be*. This is called the *progressive* form; because it expresses the continuation of action or state: *Thus*,—

Present.	*Past.*
I am loving	I was loving
Thou art loving	Thou wast loving
He is loving, &c.	He was loving, &c.

The Present and Past Indicative are also conjugated by the assistance of *do*, called the emphatic *form*: *Thus*,—

Present.	*Past.*
I do love	I did love
Thou dost love	Thou didst love
He does love, &c.	He did love, &c.

RULE I.

Verbs ending in ss, sh, ch, x, *or* o, *form the third person singular of the Present Indicative, by adding* es: *Thus*,—

He dress-es, march-es, brush-es, fix-es, go-es.

RULE II.

Verbs in y, *change* y *into* i *before the terminations* est, es, eth, *and* ed; *but not before* ing; y, *with a vowel before it, is not changed into* i: *Thus*,—

Pres. Try, triest, tries, *or* trieth.   Past. Tried.   Part. Trying.
Pres. Pray, prayest, prays, *or* prayeth. Past. Prayed. Part. Praying.

RULE III.

Verbs accented on the last syllable, and verbs of one syllable, ending in a single consonant preceded by a single vowel, double th. final consonant before the terminations est, eth, ed, ing; *but never before* s: *Thus*,—

Allot, allottest, allots, allotteth, allotted, allotting
Blot, blottest, blots, blotteth, blotted, blotting

Of Irregular Verbs.

A *regular* verb is one that forms its *past tense* and *past participle* by adding *d* or *ed* to the present: as, *Love, loved, loved.*

An *irregular* verb is one that does not form both its *past tense* and *past participle* by adding *d* or *ed* to the present; as,

Present.	*Past.*	*Past Participle*
Abide	abode	abode
Am	was	been
Arise	arose	arisen
Awake	awoke R*	awaked
Beār, *to bring forth*	bore,† bare	bôrn
Beār, *to carry*	bore, bare	bôrne
Beat	beat	beaten, *or* beat
Begin	began	begun
Bend	bent R	bent R
Bereave	bereft R	bereft R‡
Beseech	besought	besought
Bid, *for-*	bad, bäde	bidden
Bind, *un-*	bound	bound
Bite	bit	bitten, bit
Bleed	bled	bled
Blow	blew	blown
Breāk	broke	broken
Breed	bred	bred

---

* Those verbs which are conjugated regularly, as well as irregularly, are marked with an R.

† *Bore* is now more used than bare. ‡ K. 136.

Of Irregular Verbs.

Present.	Past.	Past Participle.
Bring	brought	brought
Build, *re-*	built*	built
Burst	burst	burst
Buy	bought	bought
Cast	cast	cast
Catch	caught R	caught R
Chide	chid	chidden, *or* chid
Choose	chose	chosen
Cleave, *to adhere*	clave R	cleaved
Cleave, *to split*	clove, *or* cleft	cloven, *or* cleft
Cling	clung	clung
Clothe	clothed	clad R
Come, *be-*	came	come
Cost	cost	cost
Crow	crew R	crowed
Creep	crept	crept
Cut	cut	cut
Dare, *to venture*	durst	dared
Dare, *to challenge is* R	dared	dared
Deal	dĕalt R	dĕalt R
Dig	dug, *or* digged	dug, *or* digged
Do, *mis-un-†*	did	done
Draw, *with-*	drew	drawn

---

* *Build, dwell,* and several other verbs, have the regular form *builded, dwelled, &c.*—See K. No. 135.

† The compound verbs are conjugated like the simple, by prefixing the syllables appended to them: thus, *Undo, undid, undone.*

Of IRREGULAR VERBS.

Present.	Past.	Past Participle.
Drink	drank	drunk
Drive	drove	driven
Dwell	dwelt R	dwelt R—*p.* 41
Eat	āte*	ēaten*
Fall, *be-*	fell	fallen
Feed	fed	fed
Feel	felt	felt
Fight	fought	fought
Find	found	found
Flee, *from a foe*	fled	fled
Fling	flung	flung
Fly, *as a bird*	flew	flown
Forbeār	forbore	forbōrne
Forget	forgot	forgotten, forgot
Forsake	forsook	forsaken
Freeze	froze	frozen
Get, *be-for-*	got†	got, gotten‡
Gild	gilt R	gilt R
Gird, *be-en-*	girt R	girt R
Give, *for-mis-*	gave	given
Go	went	gone
Grave, *en-* R	graved	graven
Grind	ground	ground
Grow	grew	grown

* I have excluded *eat* as the Past and Past Participle of this verb for though sometimes used by Milton and a few others, the use of it does not rest on good authority, and this verb is sufficiently irregular already.

† *Gat* and *begat* are often used in the Scriptures for *got* and *begot.*

‡ *Gotten* is nearly *obsolete.* Its compound *forgotten* is still in good use.

Of Irregular Verbs.

Present.	Past.	Past Participle
Hang	hung	hung*
Have	had	had
Hear	heard	heard
Hew, *rough-*	hewed	hewn R
Hide	hid	hidden, *or* hid
Hit	hit	hit
Hold *be-with-*	held	held
Hurt	hurt	hurt
Keep	kept	kept
Knit	knit R	knit *or* knitted
Know	knew	known
Lade	laded	laden
Lay, *in*	laid	laid
Lead, *mis*	led	led
Leave	left	left
Lend	lent	lent
Let	let	let
Lie, *to lie down*	lay	lain, *or* lien
Load	loaded	laden R
Lose	lost	lost
Make	made	made
Mean	meant	meant
Meet	met	met
Mow	mowed	mown R

---

* *Hang*, to take away life by hanging, is **regular: as, The robber was hanged, had the gone to hang up**

Of Irregular Verbs.

Present.	Past.	Past Participle.
Pay, re-	paid	paid
Put	put	put
Quit	quit, *or* quitted	quit R
Rēad	rĕad	rĕad
Rend	rent	rent
Rid	rid	rid
Ride	rode	ridden, *or* rode
Ring	rang, *or* rung*	rung
Rise, a-	rose	risen
Rive	rived	riven
Run	ran	run
Saw	sawed	sawn R
Say	said	said
See	saw	seen
Seek	sought	sought
Seethe	seethed, *or* sod	sodden
Sell	sold	sold
Send	sent	sent
Set, be	set	set
Shake	shook	shaken
Shape, *mis-*	shaped	shapen R
Shave	shaved	shaven R
Shear	shore R	shorn
Shed	shed	shed
Shine	shŏne R	shŏne R

* Where the Past might be either *ang* or *ung* &c., I have given *ang* the preference, which it certainly ought to have.

Of Irregular Verbs.

Pres.	Past.	Past Participle
Shoe	shod	shod
Shoot	shot	shot
Show*	showed	shown
Shrink	shrank, or shrunk	shrunk
Shred	shred	shred
Shut	shut	shut
Sing	sang, or sung	sung
Sink	sank, or sunk	sunk
Sit	sat	sitten, or sat†
Slay	slew	slain
Sleep	slept	slept
Slide	slid	slidden
Sling	slang, or slung	slung
Slink	slank, or slunk	slunk
Slit	slit, or slitted	slit, or slitted
Smite	smote	smitten
Sow	sowed	sown R
Speak, be-	spoke, spake	spoken
Speed	sped	sped
Spend, mis-	spent	spent
Spill	spilt R	spilt R
Spin	span, or spun	spun
Spit, be-	spat, or spit	spitten, or spit‡

---

* Or *Shew, shewed, shewn*—pronounced *show*, &c. See Note next page.

† Many authors, both here and in America, use *sate* as the Past time of *sit*; but this is improper, for it is apt to be confounded with *ate*, to glut.

‡ *Sitten* and *spitten* are preferable though obsolescent.

Of Irregular Verbs

Present.	Past.	Past Participle
Split	split	split
Spread *be-*	sprĕad	sprĕad
Spring	sprang, *or* sprung	sprung
Stand, *with-* &c.	stood	stood
Steal	stole	stolen
Stick	stuck	stuck
Sting	stung	stung
Stink	stank, *or* stunk	stunk
Stride, *be-*	strode, *or* strid	stridden [en
Strike	struck	struck, strick
String	strang, *or* strung	strung
Strive	strove	striven
Strew,* *be-*	strewed	strewed, *or* [ed
Strow	strowed	strown, strow
Swear	swore, *or* sware	swōrn
Swĕat	swĕat	swĕat
Sweep	swept	swept
Swell	swelled	swollen n
Swim	swam, *or* swum	swum
Swing	swang, *or* swung	swung
Take, *be-* &c.	took	taken
Teach, *mis-re-*	taught	taught
Tear, *un-*	tore	tōrn
Tell	told	told

* *Strew* and *shew* are now giving way to *strow* and *show*, as they are pronounced

Of Irregular Verbs.

Present.	Past.	Past Participle
Think, be-	thought	thought
Thrive	throve	thriven
Throw	threw	thrown
Thrust	thrust	thrust
Tread	trod	trodden
Wax	waxed	waxen R
Wear	wore	worn
Weave	wove	woven
Weep	wept	wept
Win	won	won
Wind	wound	wound
Work	wrought R	wrought, worked
Wring	wrung	wrung
Write	wrote	written

Defective verbs are those which want some of their moods and tenses.

Present.	Past.	Past Participle.	Present.	Past.	Past Participle.
Can,	could,	———	Shall,	should,	———
May,	might,	———	Will,	would,	———
Must,	must,	———	Wis,	wist,	———
Ought,	ought,	———	Wit or Wot,	wot,	———
———	quoth.				

EXERCISES ON THE IRREGULAR VERBS.

Name the Past Tense and Past Participle of

Take, drive, creep, begin, abide, buy, bring, rise, catch, bereave, am, burst, draw, drink, fly, flee, fall, get, give, go, feel, forsake, grow, have, hear, hide, keep, know, lose, pay, ride, ring, shake, run, seek, sell, see, sit, slay, slide.

Of Adverbs.

An *adverb* is a word joined to a *verb*, an *adjective*, or another *adverb*, to express some quality or circumstance of *time*, *place*, or *manner*, respecting it; as, Ann speaks *distinctly*, she is *remarkably* diligent, and reads *very correctly*.

A LIST OF ADVERBS.

* So, no, not, nay, yea, yes, too, well, up, very, forth, how, why, far, now, then, ill, soon, much, here, there, where, when, whence, thence, still, †more, most, little, less, least, thus, since, ever, never, while, whilst, once, twice, thrice, first, scarcely, quite, rather, again, ago, seldom, often, indeed, exceedingly, already, hither, thither, whether, doubtless, hardly, perhaps, enough, daily, always, sometimes, almost, alone, peradventure, backward, forward, upward, downward, together, apart, asunder, viz., to and fro, in fine.

OBSERVATIONS

* *As* and *so*, without a corresponding *as* or *so*, are adverbs.

The generality of these words that end in *ly*, are adverbs of manner or quality. They are formed from adjectives by adding *ly*; as from *foolish* comes *foolishly*.

The compounds of *here*, *there*, *where*, and *wither*, *thither*, and *whither*, are all adverbs; except *therefore* and *wherefore*, occasionally conjunctions.

Some adverbs are compared like adjectives: as, *often*, *oftener*, *oftenest*. Such words as *ashore*, *afoot*, *aground*, &c., are all adverbs.

† When *more* and *most* qualify nouns they are *adjectives*; but in every other situation they are *adverbs*.

An adjective, when a preposition before it, is by some called an adverb; as, *in general*, *in haste*, &c., i. e. *generally*, *hastily*.—It would be a piece of vexatious refinement to make children, in parsing, call *in general*, an adverb, instead of *in* a preposition—*general*, an adjective, having *way* or *view* understood. That such phrases are convertible into adverbs is not a good reason for calling them so.

There are many words that are sometimes used as *adverbs*; as, I am *more* afraid than ever; and sometimes as *adjectives*; as, He has *more* wealth than wisdom.—See next page

Exercises on ADVERBS, IRREGULAR VERBS, &c.

Immediately the cock crew. Peter wept bitterly. He is here now. She went away yesterday.* They came to-day. They will perhaps buy some to-morrow. Ye shall know hereafter. She sung sweetly. Cats soon learn to† catch mice. Mary rose up hastily. They that have enough‡ may soundly sleep. Cain wickedly slew his brother. I saw him long ago. He is a very good man. Sooner or later all must die. You read too little. They talk too much. James acted wisely. How many lines can you repeat? You ran hastily. He speaks fluently. Then were they glad. He fell fast asleep. She should not hold her head a-wry. The ship was driven ashore. No, indeed. They are all alike. Let him that is athirst drink freely. The oftener you read attentively, the more you will improve.

OBSERVATIONS.

* *To-day, yesterday,* and *to-morrow,* are always nouns, for they are parts of time; as, *Yesterday* is past, *to-day* is passing, and we may never see *to-morrow.*—When these words answer to the question *when,* they are governed by a preposition *understood*; as, When will John come home? (on) *to-morrow,* for he went away (on) *yesterday.*

Much is used, 1. As an *adverb*; as, It is *much* better to give than to receive.
    2. As an *adjective*; as, In *much* wisdom is *much* grief.
    3. As a *noun*; as, Where *much* is given *much* is required.

In strict propriety, however, *much* can never be a noun, but an *adjective*; for were the question to be asked, *Much what* is given? it would be necessary to add a *noun,* and say, Where *much grace* is given, *much gratitude* is required.

† *To,* before the infinite of verbs, is an adverb, according to Johnson, and according to Murray, a preposition. The *two together* may be called the infinitive.

‡ *Enough* (a sufficiency) is here a noun. Its plural, *enow,* is applied, like *many,* to things that are numbered. *Enough,* an adjective, like *much,* should perhaps be applied only to things that are weighed or measured.

Of Prepositions.

A *Preposition* is a word put before nouns and pronouns, to show the relation between them; as, He sailed *from* Leith *to* London *in* two days.

A LIST OF PREPOSITIONS.
To be got accurately by heart.

About, above, according to, across, after, against, along, amid, amidst, among, amongst, around, at, athwart. Bating, before, behind, below, beneath, besides, beside, between, betwixt, beyond, by. Concerning. Down, during. Except, excepting. For, from. In, into, instead of. Near, nigh. Of, off, on, over, out of. Past. Regarding, respecting, round. Since. Through, throughout, till, to, touching, towards.* Under, underneath, unto, up, upon. With, within, without.

OBSERVATIONS.

Every preposition requires an objective case after it.—When a preposition does not govern an objective case, it becomes an adverb; as, He rides *about*. But in such phrases as, *cast up, hold out, fall on,* the words *up, out,* and *on,* must be considered as a part of the verb, rather than as prepositions or adverbs.

Some words are used as prepositions in one place, and as adverbs in another, thus, *before* is a preposition when it refers to *place*; as, He stood *before* the door; and an adverb when it refers to *time*, as, *Before* that Philip called thee, I saw thee. The word *before,* however, and others in similar situations, may still be considered as prepositions, if we supply an appropriate noun; as, *Before* the *time* that Philip, &c.

* *Towards* is a preposition, but *toward* is an adjective, and means, "Ready to do or learn; compliant with duty; not froward." *Toward* is sometimes improperly used for *towards*.

The *Inseparable* Prepositions are omitted, because an explanation of them can impart no information without a previous knowledge of the radical word. Suppose the pupil told that *con* means *together,* will this explain *convene* to him? No: he must first be told that *vene* signifies to come, and then CON, *together*. Would it not be better to tell him at once that *convene* means to *come* or *call together*?

Some grammarians distribute adverbs into classes; such as adverbs of *negation, affirmation,* &c.; prepositions into *separable* and *inseparable;* and conjunctions into seven classes, besides the we mentioned next page. Such a classification has been omitted here, because its utility is questionable.

Of Conjunctions.

A *Conjunction* is a word which joins words and sentences together; as, You *and* I must go to Leith; *but* Peter may stay at home.

A LIST OF CONJUNCTIONS

Copulative.—Also, and, because, both, for,* if, since, that, then, therefore, wherefore.

Disjunctive.—Although, as, as well as, but, either, except, lest, neither, nor, notwithstanding, or, provided, so, than, though, unless, whether, yet.

EXERCISES ON CONJUNCTIONS, &c.

Though he was rich, yet for our sakes he became poor. Blessed are the meek; for they shall inherit the earth. The life is more than meat, and the body is more than raiment Consider the ravens; for they neither sow nor reap; which have neither store-house nor barn; and God feedeth them. You are happy, because you are good.

OBSERVATIONS.

* When *for* can be turned into *because*, it is a *conjunction.*

Several words which are marked as adverbs in Johnson's Dictionary, are in many Grammars marked as conjunctions; such as, *Albeit, else, moreover, likewise, otherwise, nevertheless, then, therefore, wherefore.* Whether they be called adverbs or conjunctions, it signifies but little.

But, in some cases, is an *adverb;* as, "We are *but* (only) of yesterday, and know nothing."

Sometimes the same words are used as conjunctions in one place, and as prepositions or adverbs in another place; as, *Since* (conj.) we must part, let us do it peaceably; I have not seen him *since* (prep.) that time; Our friendship commenced long *since* (adv.)†

† As many distinctions, however proper in themselves, may prove more hurtful than useful, they should not be made till the learner be perfectly acquainted with the more obvious facts.

Of Interjections.

An *Interjection* is a word which expresses some emotion of the speaker; as, *Oh*, what a sight is here! *Well done!*

A LIST OF INTERJECTIONS.

Adieu! ah! alas! alack! away! aha! begone! hark! ho! ha! he! hail! halloo! hum! hush! huzza! hist! hey-day! lo! O! O strange! O brave! *pshaw*. see! well-a-day, &c

CORRECT THE FOLLOWING ERRORS.

I saw a boy which is blind."
I saw a flock of gooses.
This is the horse who was lost.
This is the hat whom I wear.
John is here; she is a good boy.
The hen lays his eggs.
Jane is here; he reads well.
I saw two mouses.
The dog follows her master.
This two horses eat hay.
John met three mans
We saw two childs.
He has but one teeth.
The well is ten foot deep.
Look at the oxes.
This horse will let me ride on her.
I can stay this two hours.
I have two pen-knifes.
My lady has got his fan.
Two pair of ladies's gloves
Henry the Eighth had six wi'es.
I saw the man which sings.
We saw an ass who brayed at us.
They will stay this two days.

We was not there."
loves him.
He love me
Thou have been busy.
He dare not speak.
She need not do it.
Was you there?
You was not there.
We was sorry for it.
Thou might not go.
He dost not learn.
If I does that.
Thou may do it.
You was never there
The book were lost.
Thou will better stop.
The horses was sold.
The boys was reading.
I teaches him grammar
He are not attentive to it
Thou shall not go out.
If I sees not at home.
Thou can do nothing for me.
John need not go now.

These exercises will at once amuse and improve the pupil. -
ee Syntax, Rule 14 and 15.

† Syntax, Rule 1

ON PARSING.

Having the exercises on Parsing* and Syntax in *one* volume with the Grammar, is a *convenience* so exceedingly great, that it must be obvious. The following set of exercises on Parsing are arranged on a plan *new* and important.

All the most material points, and those that are apt to puzzle the pupil, have been selected, and made the subject of a whole page of exercises, and, where very important, of two. By this means, the same point must come so often under his eye, and be so often repeated, that it cannot fail to make a strong impression on his mind; and even should he forget it, it will be easy to refresh his memory by turning to it again.

To give full scope to the pupil's discriminating powers, the exercises contain all the parts of speech, promiscuously arranged, to be used thus:—

1. After the pupil has got the definition of a noun, exercise him in going over any part of the exercises in parsing, and pointing out the NOUNS *only*. This will oblige him to exercise his powers of discrimination, in distinguishing the nouns from the *other* words.†

2. After getting the definition of an adjective, exercise him in selecting all the *adjectives* from the other words, and telling *why* they are adjectives.

3. After getting all the *pronouns* very accurately by heart, let him point out them, in addition to the nouns and adjectives.

4. Then the *verb*, without telling what *sort*, or what *number* or *person*, or *tense*, for several weeks, or longer, till he can distinguish it with great readiness.

5. Then the definition of an *adverb*, after which exercise him *orally* with many short sentences containing adverbs, and then on those in the book.

---

* *Parse* should be pronounced *parce*, and not *purz.*—See Key, p 7˚

† Those accustomed to use Mr. Murray's lessons in parsing, will perhaps think the following too difficult; let such, however, reflect, that Mr. Murray's are too easy; for when no other words are introduced than an *article* and a *noun*, no exercise is given to the pupil's judgement at all, for in every sentence he finds only an *article* and a *noun*; and in the next *set* only an *article*, an *adjective*, and a *noun*, and so on. There is no room for discrimination here, and yet discrimination is the very thing he should be taught.

6. Get all the prepositions by heart, for it is impossible to give such a definition of a preposition as will lead a child to distinguish it with certainty from every other sort of word.

7. Get all the conjunctions by heart. They have been alphabetically arranged, like the prepositions, to facilitate the committing of them to memory.

8. After this, the pupil, if very young, may go over all the exercises, by parsing every word in the most simple manner, viz., by saying such a word, a *noun, singular*, without telling its *gender* and *case*; such a word, a *verb*, without telling its *nature, number, person, tense*, and *mood*.

9. In the next and last course, he should go over the exercises, and tell *every* thing about *nouns* and *verbs*, &c., as shown in the example below.

☞ In the Exercises on Parsing, the *sentences* on every page are numbered by small *figures*, to enable the reader to find out any sentence in the Key which he may wish to consult.

The small *letters* refer to the Nos. For example, *p.* in the first sentence of No. *s.*, directs the learner to turn to No. *p.* page 74, and remark that it says, "The verb *to be*, or *to have*, is often *understood;*" intimating to him by this reference, that *to be* is understood after *man* in the first sentence of No. *s.*

    O how stupendous was the power
    That raised me with a word
    And every day and every hour
    I lean upon the Lord.

O, an interjection—*how*, an adverb—*stupendous* an adjective, in the positive degree, compared by more and most; as, stupendous, more stupendous, most stupendous—*was*, a verb neuter, third person singular, past indicative, (*agreeing with its nominative *power*, here put after it)—*the*, an article, the definite—*power*, a noun, singular, neuter, the nominative—*that*, a relative pronoun, singular, neuter, the nominative, here used for *which*; its antecedent is *power*—*raised*, a verb, active, third person, singular, past, indicative, (agreeing with its nominative *that*)—*me*, the first personal pronoun, singular, masculine, or feminine, the objective, (governed by *raised*)—*with*, a preposition—*a*, an article, the indefinite—*word*, a noun, singular, neuter, the objective, (governed by *with*)—*and*, a conjunction—*every*, a distributive pronoun—*day*, a noun, singular, neuter, the objective, (because the preposition *through* or *during* is understood,) *and*, and *every*, as before—*hour*, a noun, singular, neuter, the objective, (because day was in it, and conjunctions couple the same cases of nouns, &c.)—*I*, the first personal pronoun, singular, masculine, or feminine, the nominative—*lean*, a verb, neuter, first person singular, present, indicative—*upon*, a preposition—*the*, an article, the definite—*Lord*, a noun, singular, masculine, the objective, (governed by *upon*.)

---

* Omit the words within the ( ) till the pupil get the rules of Syntax

EXERCISES IN PARSING.

A few easy sentences chiefly intended as an Exercise on the Active Verb; but to be previously used as an Exercise on Nouns and Adjectives.

No. a.

A good conscience and a contented mind will make a man*ᵖ* happy.¹ Philosophy teaches us to endure afflictions, but Christianity*ᵖ** to enjoy them, by turning them into blessings.² Virtue ennobles the mind, but vice debases it.³ Application, in the early period of life, will give happiness and ease to succeeding years.⁴ A good conscience fears nothing.⁵ Devotion promotes and strengthens virtue, calms and regulates the temper; and fills the heart with gratitude and praise.⁶ Dissimulation degrades parts and learning, obscures the lustre of every accomplishment, and sinks us into universal contempt.⁷

If we lay no restraint upon our lusts, no control upon our appetites and passions, they will hurry us into guilt and misery.⁸ Discretion stamps a value upon all our other qualities; it instructs us to make use of them at proper times, and turns them honourably to our own advantage: it shows itself alike in all our words and actions, and serves as an unerring guide in every occurrence of life.⁹ Shame and disappointment attend sloth and idleness.¹⁰ Indolence undermines the foundation of every virtue, and unfits a man for the social duties of life.¹¹

---

* Supply *teaches us*, as a reference to No. *p.* Intimates.—See ☞ on the preceding page. See *Key,* page 75, &c.

EXERCISES IN PARSING.
Chiefly on the Active Verb—Continued from last page.

No. a.

Knowledge gives ease to solitude, and grace fulness to retirement.[12] Gentleness ought to form our address, to regulate our speech, and to diffuse itself over our whole behaviour.[13] Knowledge makes our being pleasant to us, fills the mind with entertaining views, and administers to it a perpetual series of gratifications.[14] Meekness controls our angry passions; candour our severe judgements.[15] Perseverance in labour will surmount every difficulty.[16] He that takes pleasure in the prosperity of others enjoys part of their good fortune.[17] Restlessness of mind disqualifies us both for the enjoyment of our peace, and the performance of our duty.[18] Sadness contracts the mind; mirth dilates it.[19]

We should subject our fancies to the government of reason.[20] Self-conceit, presumption, and obstinacy, blast the prospect of many a youth.[21] Affluence may give us respect in the eyes of the vulgar; but it will not recommend us to the wise and good.[22] Complaisance produces good nature and mutual benevolence encourages the timorous, and soothes the turbulent.[23] A constant perseverance in the paths of virtue will gain respect.[24] Envy and wrath shorten life; and anxiety bringeth age before its time.[25] Bad habits require immediate reformation.[26]

EXERCISES IN PARSING.

Chiefly on the Neuter Verb, including the verb *To be*

No. b.

Economy is no disgrace: it is better to live on a little,[2] than to outlive[a] a great deal.[1] A virtuous education is a better inheritance than a great estate.[2] Good and wise men only can be real friends.[3] Friendship can scarcely exist where virtue is not the foundation.[4] He that[i] swells in prosperity, will shrink in adversity.[5] To despair[a] in adversity is madness.[6] From idleness arises[a] neither pleasure nor advantage. we must flee therefore from idleness,[a] the certain parent of guilt and ruin.[7]

You must not always rely on promises.[8] The peace of society dependeth on justice.[9] He that[i] walketh with wise men shall be wise.[10] He that[i] sitteth with the profane is foolish.[11] The coach arrives daily.[12] The mail travels fast.[13] Rain falls in great abundance here.[14] He sleeps soundly.[15] She dances gracefully.[16] I went to York.[17] He lives soberly.[18] He hurried to his house in the country.[19] They smiled.[20] She laughed.[21]* He that[i] liveth in pleasure is dead while he liveth.[22] Nothing appears to be[m] so low and mean as lying and dissimulation.[23] Vice is its own punishment, and virtue is its own reward.[24] Industry is the road to wealth, and virtue[p] to happiness.[25]

---

* These verbs would be active, were a preposition joined to them. Thus, "she *smiled at* him," "she *smiled upon* him;" "she *laughs at* me." In this case, the preposition must be considered as a *part* of the verb.

EXERCISES IN PARSING.

Chiefly on the Passive Verb—See page, 35, *bottom.*

No. c.

Virtue must be formed and supported by daily and repeated exertions.[1] You may be deprived of honour and riches against your will; but[2] not of virtue without your consent.[2] Virtue is connected with eminence in every liberal art.[3] Many are brought to ruin by extravagance and dissipation.[4] The best designs are often ruined by unnecessary delay.[5] All our recreations should be accompanied with virtue and innocence.[6] Almost all difficulties may be overcome by diligence.[7] Old friends are preserved, and new ones are procured, by a grateful disposition.[8] Words are like arrows, and should not be shot at random.[9]

A desire to be thought learned* often prevents our improvement.[10] Great merit is often concealed under the most unpromising appearances.[11] Some talents are buried in the earth, and others are properly employed.[12] Much mischief has often been prevented by timely consideration.[13] True pleasure is only to be found in the paths of virtue; and every deviation from them will be attended with pain.[14] That† friend is highly to be respected at all times, whose friendship is chiefly distinguished in adversity.[15]

---

* *Learned*, here, is an adjective, and should be pronounced, *learn-ed*
Concerning *that*, see Notes, p. 17.

EXERCISES IN PARSING.

Chiefly of the Passive Verb—Continued.

No. c.

There is not a more pleasing exercise of the mind than gratitude: it is accompanied with such an inward satisfaction, that the duty is sufficiently rewarded by the performance.[16] The mind should be stored with knowledge and cultivated with care.[17] A pardon was obtained for him from the king.[18] Our most sanguine prospects have often been blasted.[19] Too sanguine hopes of any earthly thing should never be entertained.[20] The table of Dionysius the tyrant was loaded with delicacies of every kind, yet he could not eat."[21] I have long been taught, that the afflictions of this life are overpaid by that eternal weight of glory which awaits the virtuous."[22]

Greater virtue is required to bear good fortune than bad.[23] Riches and honour have always been reserved for the good.[24] King Alfred is said to have divided the day and night into three parts: eight hours were allotted for meals and sleep,—eight were allotted for business and recreation, and eight for study and devotion.[25] All our actions should be regulated by religion and reason.[26] Honours, monuments, and all the works of vanity and ambition, are demolished and destroyed by time; but the reputation of wisdom is transmitted to posterity.[27] These two things cannot be disjoined; a pious life and a happy death.[28]

EXERCISES IN PARSING.
Different sorts of Verbs in the Imperative.

No. d.

Forget the faults of others, and remember your own.[1] Study universal rectitude, and cherish religious hope.[2] Suit your desires to things, and not things to your desires.[3] Cherish virtuous principles, and be ever steady in your conduct.[4] Practise humility, and reject every thing in dress, carriage, or conversation, which has any appearance of pride.[5] Allow nothing to interrupt your public or private devotions, except the performance of some humane action.[6]

"Learn to contemn all praise betimes,
For* flattery is the nurse of crimes."[7]

Consider yourself[r] a citizen of the world; and deem nothing which[s] regards humanity unworthy of your notice.[8] Presume[5] not in prosperity, and despair[6] not in adversity.[9] Be kind and courteous to all, and be not eager[m] to take offence without just reason.[10] Beware[6] of ill customs; they creep[6] upon us insidiously, and by slow degrees.[11]

"Oh man, degenerate man, offend no more!
Go† learn of brutes, thy Maker to adore!"[12]

Let your religion‡ connect preparation for heaven with an honourable discharge of the duties of active life.[13] Let your words‡ agree with your thoughts, and‡ be followed by your actions.[14]

---

* See Note *First*, p. 51.
† *Go* and *learn* are both in the *imperative.*—‡ See *Note,* next page

EXERCISES IN PARSING.
Different sorts of Verbs in the Imperative—Continued.*

No. d.

Let all your thoughts, words, and actions, be tinctured* with humility, modesty, and candour.[15] Let him who wishes for an effectual cure to all the wounds the world can inflict,* retire from intercourse with men to intercourse with his Creator.[16]

Let no reproach make you* lay aside holiness; the frowns of the world are nothing to the smiles of heaven.[17] Let reason go before enterprise, and counsel before every action.[18] Hear Ann read her lesson.[19] Bid her get it better.[20] You need not hear her again.[21] I perceive her weep.[22] I feel it pain me.[23] I dare not go.[24] You behold him run.[25] We observed him walk off hastily.[26]

And that tongue of his, that bade the Romans
Mark* him, and write his speeches in their books.
Alas! it cried—give* me some drink, Titinius.*

Deal with another as you'd have
Another* deal with you;
What you're unwilling to receive,
Be sure you never do.[28]

Abstain from pleasure and bear evil.[29] Expect the same filial duty from your children which you paid to your parents.[30]

---

* The next verb after *bid, dare, need, make, see, hear, feel, let, perceive, behold, observe, have* and *known*, is in the *Infinitive*, having *to* understood: as, "The tempest-loving raven scarce dares (to) wing the dubious dusk."—I have *known* him (to) *divert* the money, &c. *To* is often used after the compound tenses of these verbs; as, Who will dare *to* advance, if I say -stop? Them did he make *to* pay tribute

EXERCISES IN PARSING.

The Nominative, though generally placed *before* the verb, is often placed *after* it; especially when the sentence begins with *Here*, *there*, &c., or when *if* or *though* is understood; and when a question is asked.

No. e.

Among the many enemies of friendship may be reckoned suspicion and disgust.[1] Among the great blessings and wonders of the creation may be classed the regularities of times and seasons.[2] Then were they in great fear.[3] Here stands the oak.[4] And there sat in a window a certain young man named Eutychus.[5] Then shall thy light break forth as the morning.[6] Then shalt thou see clearly.[7] Where is thy brother?[8] Is he at home?[9]

There are delivered in Holy Scripture many weighty arguments for this doctrine.[10] Were he at leisure, I would wait upon him.[11] Had he been more prudent, he would have been more fortunate.[12] Were they wise, they would read the Scriptures daily.[13] I would give more[r2] to the poor, were I able.[14] Could we survey the chambers of sickness and distress, we should often find them[p] peopled with the victims of intemperance, sensuality, indolence, and sloth.[15] Were he to assert it, I would not believe it, because he told a lie before.[16] Gaming is a vice[p] pregnant with every evil; and to it are often sacrificed wealth, happiness, and every thing virtuous and valuable.[17] Is not industry the road to wealth, and[p] virtue[p] to happiness?[18]

EXERCISES IN PARSING.
The Nominative is often at a great distance from the verb.

No. f.

That man' who is neither elated by success nor dejected by disappointment, whose conduct is not influenced by any change of circumstances to deviate from the line of integrity, possesses true fortitude of mind.¹ That fortitude which has encountered no dangers, that prudence which has surmounted no difficulties, that integrity which has been attacked by no temptations,—can at best be considered but as gold, not yet" brought to the test, of which, therefore, the true value cannot be assigned.²

The man' who retires to meditate mischief, and to exasperate his own rage; whose thoughts are employed only on means of distress, and contrivances of ruin; whose mind never pauses' from the remembrance of his own sufferings, but to indulge some hope of enjoying the calamities of another; may justly be numbered among the most miserable of human beings; among those who are" guilty without reward: who have neither the gladness of prosperity nor the calm of innocence.³ He whose constant employment is detraction and censure; who looks only to find faults, and speaks only to publish them; will be dreaded, hated, and avoided.

> He! who through vast immensity can pierce,
> See worlds on worlds*²* compose one universe,
> Observe how system into system runs,
> What*f* other planets circle other suns,
> What varied being peoples every star,
> May tell why Heaven has made us as we are'

EXERCISES IN PARSING.

The Infinitive, or part of a sentence, being equal to a noun, is often the nominative to a verb.

No. 9.

To be ashamed of the practice of precepts which*a* the heart approves and embraces, from a fear of the censure of the world,* marks a feeble and imperfect character.¹ To endure misfortune with resignation, and bear it with fortitude, is¹⁸ᵗ the striking characteristic of a great mind.² To rejoice in the welfare of our fellow creatures, is, in a degree, to partake of their good fortune; but to repine at their prosperity, is one of the most despicable traits of a narrow mind.³

To be ever active in laudable pursuits, is the distinguishing characteristic of a man of merit.⁴ To satisfy all his demands, is the way to make your child*p* truly miserable.⁵ To practise virtue is the sure way to love it.⁶ To be at once merry and malicious, is the sign of a corrupt heart and a weak understanding.⁷ To bear adversity well is difficult, but to be temperate in prosperity is the height of wisdom.⁸ To advise the ignorant, relieve the needy, and comfort the afflicted,† are duties that fall in our way, almost every day of our lives.⁹ To dread no eye, and to suspect no tongue, is¹⁸ᵗ the great prerogative of innocence.¹⁰

---

* When nothing but an infinitive precedes the verb, then it is the *infinitive* that is the nominative to it: as, *To play* is pleasant. But when the infinitive has any *adjuncts*, as in the sentence, *To drink poison* is death, it is the part of a sentence; for it is not *to drink* that is death, but *to drink poison.*

† *Two* or more infinitives require a verb in the plural.—See R. 18, b.

EXERCISES IN PARSING.

The relative is the nominative to the verb, when it stands immediately before the verb.—When not close to the verb, it is in the objective, and governed by the verb that comes *after* it, or by a preposition.*

No. *h.*

The value of any possession is to be chiefly estimated, by the relief which it can bring us in the time of our greatest need.¹ The veil which covers from our sight the events of succeeding years, is a veil° woven by the hand of mercy.² The chief misfortunes that befall us in life can be traced to some vices or follies which we have committed.³ Beware⁴ of those rash and dangerous connections which may afterwards load you with dishonour.⁴ True charity is not a meteor which* occasionally glances, but a luminary, which,* in its orderly and regular course, dispenses a benignant influence.⁵

We usually find that to be the sweetest fruit, which the birds have picked.⁶ Wealth cannot confer greatness; for nothing can make that ʳgreat, which the decree of nature has ordained to be little.⁷ Justice consists not merely in performing those duties which the laws of society oblige us to perform, but in our duty to our Maker, to others, and to ourselves.⁸ True religion will show its influence in every part of our conduct; it is like the sap† of a living tree, which pervades the most distant boughs.⁹

---
* An *adverb*, or a *clause* between *two commas*, frequently comes between the relative and the verb.—The rule at the top is but a *general rule*: for in Poetry, in particular, the *Relative*, though not close to the verb, is sometimes in the nominative —*See* first line of Poetry, p. 63.

† *Sap,* the *obj.* governed by *to* understood after *like,* and antec. to *which.*

EXERCISES IN PARSING.

When the antecedent and relative are *both* in the *nominative*, the relative is the nominative to the verb *next* it, and the antecedent is generally the nominative to the *second* verb.

No. 1.

He who performs every part of his business in its due place and season, suffers no part of time to escape without profit.[1] He that does good for the sake of virtue, seeks neither praise nor reward, though he is sure of both at the last.[2] He that is the abettor of a bad action, is equally guilty with him that commits it.[3] He that overcomes his passions, conquers his greatest enemies.[4] The consolation which is derived from a reliance upon Providence, enables us to support the most severe misfortunes.[5]

That wisdom which enlightens the understanding and reforms the life, is the most valuable.[6] Those and those only, who have felt the pleasing influence of the most genuine and exalted friendship, can comprehend its beauties.[7] An error that proceeds from any good principle, leaves no room for resentment.[8] Those who raise envy will easily incur censure.[9] He who is a stranger to industry, may possess, but he cannot enjoy; he only who is active and industrious, can experience real pleasure.[10] That man who is neither elated by success, nor dejected by disappointment, whose conduct is not influenced by any change of circumstances to deviate from the line of integrity, possesses true fortitude of mind.[11]

EXERCISES IN PARSING.

That is equal to—*that which*—or *the thing which*—and represents two cases;—sometimes two *nominatives*;—sometimes two *objectives*;—sometimes a nominative and an objective;—and sometimes an objective and a nominative.—Sometimes it is an *adjective*

No. 7.

Regard the quality, rather than the quantity of what you read. If we delay till to-morrow what ought to be done*,*[a, b] to-day, we overcharge the to-morrow with a burden which belongs not to it.[2] Choose what is most fit: custom will make it the most agreeable.[3] Foolish men are more apt to consider what they have lost, than what they possess, and to turn their eyes on those who are richer than themselves, rather than on those who are under greater difficulties.[4]

What cannot be mended or prevented, must be endured.[5] Be attentive to what you are about, and take pains to do it well.[6] What you do not hear to-day, you will not tell to-morrow.[7] Mark Antony, when under adverse circumstances, made this interesting remark, "I have lost all, except what I gave away."[8] Mark what it is his mind aims at in the question, and not what* words* he utters.[9]

By what* means shall I obtain wisdom?
See what* a grace was seated on his brow![10]

---

* *What* here, and generally in questions, is an adjective, like *many* in "many a flower."—Sometimes it is an *interjection*; as, *What!*

What is sometimes used as an *adverb* for *partly*; thus, *What* with thinking, *what* with writing, and *what* with reading, I am weary

EXERCISES IN PARSING.

The compound relatives,—*whoever* and *whosoever*—are equal to—*he who*.

Whatever and *whatsoever*, are equal to—*the thing which*,—and represent two cases like *which*, as on the preceding page.—*See page 16, last two notes.*

No. k.

Whatever gives pain to others, deserves not the name of pleasure.[1] Whoever lives under an habitual sense of the divine presence, keeps up a perpetual cheerfulness of temper.[2] Whatsoever is set before you, eat.[3] Aspire after perfection in* whatever state of life you choose.[4] Whoever is not content in poverty, would not be so in plenty; for the fault is not in the thing, but in the mind.[5] Whatever is worth doing, is worth doing well.[6]

*By whatever arts you may at first attract the attention, you can hold the esteem, and secure the hearts of others, only by amiable dispositions, and the accomplishments of the mind.[7] Whatever delight, or whatever solace is granted by the celestials to soften our fatigues—in thy presence, O Health, thou parent of happiness! all those joys spread out and flourish.[8] *Whatever your situation in life may be, nothing is more necessary to your success, than the acquirement of virtuous dispositions and habits.[9] *Whatever be the motive of insult, it is always best to overlook it and revenge it in no circumstances whatever.[1]

---

* *Whatever* is an *adjective* here, for it qualifies *arts*, &c.; and where no noun is after it, it agrees with *thing* understood. Thus, *Whatever may be the motive, &c.*, that is, *Whatever thing may be*

EXERCISES IN PARSING

Do, did, and *have,* are auxiliary verbs when joined to the verb; but when not joined to another verb, they are principal verbs, and have auxiliaries like the verb to *love.*

No. 1.

He who does not perform what he has promised is a traitor to his friend.¹ Earthly happiness does not flow from riches; but from content of mind, health of body, and a life of piety and virtue.² Examples do not authorize a fault.³ If we do not study the Scriptures, they will never make us wise.⁴ The butler did not remember Joseph.⁵ You did not get enough of time to prepare your lessons.⁶ Did you see my book?⁷ Do you go to-morrow?⁸ I do not think it proper to play too long.⁹ Did he deceive you?¹⁰ He did deceive me.¹¹ I do not hate my enemies.¹² Wisdom does not make a man proud.¹³

Principal.—He who does the most good,* has the most pleasure.¹⁴ Instead of adding to the afflictions of others, do whatever you can to alleviate them.¹⁵ If ye do these things, ye shall never fall.¹⁶ If thou canst do anything, have compassion on us, and help us.¹⁷ He did his work well.¹⁸ Did he do his work well?¹⁹ Did you do what I requested you to do?²⁰ Deceit betrays a littleness of mind, and is the resource of one who has not courage to avow his failings.²¹ We have no bread.²²

---

* *Have, hast, has, hath, had,* and *hadst,* are auxiliaries only when they have the Past Participle of another verb after them.

EXERCISES IN PARSING.

The verb to be *has very often an objective after it, and some adjectives seem so closely connected with it, as to lead young people to suppose that they have got a passive verb.*

No. III.

Prudence and moderation are productive of true peace and comfort.[1] If the powers of reflection were cultivated* by habit, mankind would at all times be able to derive pleasure from their own breasts, as rational as it is exalted.[2] Learning is preferable to riches; but virtue is preferable to both.[3] He who rests on a principle within, is incapable of betraying his trust or deserting his friend.[4] Saul was afraid of David.[5] And the men were afraid.[6] One would have thought she should have been contented.[7]

Few things are impracticable in themselves.[8] To study without intermission is impossible relaxation is necessary; but it should be moderate.[9] The Athenians were conceited on account of their own wit, science, and politeness.[10] We are indebted to our ancestors for our civil and religious liberty.[11] Many things are worth inquiry to one man, which are not so to another.[12] An idle person is a kind of monster in the creation, because all nature is busy about him.[13] Impress your minds with reverence for all that is sacred.[14] He was unfortunate, because he was inconsiderate.[15] She is conscious of her deficiency, and will therefore be busy.[16] I am ashamed of you.[17] She is sadly forlorn.[18]

---

* Were cultivated, a verb passive.

EXERCISES IN PARSING.

1. Active and neuter verbs are often conjugated with their *Present Participle* joined to the verb *to be.*
2. A noun is always understood, when not expressed, after Adjectives, and Adjective Pronouns; such as, *few, many, this, that, all, such, every, either.*—See p. 145, under *They, those.*

No. 11.

1. While I am reading, you should be listening to what I read.[1] He was delivering his speech when I left the house.[2] They have been writing on botany.[3] He might have been rising to eminence.[4] I have been writing a letter, and I am just going to send it away.[5] She was walking by herself when I met her.[6] We are perishing with hunger; I am willing therefore to surrender.[7] We should always be learning.[8] A good man is always studying to be better.[9] We were hearing a sermon yesterday.[10]

2. These only are truly great who are really good.[11] Few set a proper value on their time.[12] Those who despise the admonitions of their friends, deserve the mischiefs which[*] their own obstinacy brings upon them.[13] Among the many social virtues which attend the practice of true religion, that of a strict adherence to truth is of the greatest importance.[14] Love no interests but those of truth and virtue.[15] Such as are diligent will be rewarded.[16] I saw a thousand.[17] Of all prodigality, that of time is the worst.[18] Some are naturally timid; and some bold and active; for all are not alike.[19]

---

* Many words both in *ing* and *ed* are mere adjectives.

EXERCISES IN PARSING.

The *Past Participle* has uniformly either a relative or personal pronoun, with some part of the verb *to be* understood before it.*

No. 9.

Make the study of the sacred Scriptures¹ your daily practice and concern; and embrace the doctrines contained in them, as the real oracles of Heaven, and the dictates of that Spirit that cannot lie.¹ Knowledge softened with complacency and good-breeding, will make a man beloved and admired.² Gratitude and thanks are the least returns which children can make to their parents for the numberless obligations conferred on them.³ Precepts have little influence when not enforced by example.⁴ He is of all human beings the happiest who has a conscience† untainted by guilt, and a mind so well† regulated as to be able to accommodate itself to whatever the wisdom of Heaven shall think fit to ordain.⁵ Mere external beauty is of little estimation; and deformity, when associated with amiable dispositions and useful qualities, does¹ not preclude our respect and approbation.⁶ True honour, as defined by Cicero, is the concurrent approbation of good men.⁷ Modesty seldom resides in a breast not enriched with nobler virtues.⁸

---

* It is often difficult to supply the *right* part of the verb *to be*. An *adverb* is often understood. The *scope* of the passage must determine what part of *to be*, and what *adverb*, when an adverb is necessary, should be supplied; for no general rule for this can be given.

☞ The Past *Tense* has always a nom. either expressed or easily understood: but the Past *Part*. has no nom.—See *Key*, p. 81, No. 16.

† *Untainted* and *regulated* are adjectives here.

EXERCISES IN PARSING.

On the Past Participle—Continued from last page.

No. 9.

An elevated genius, employed in little things, appears like the sun in his evening declination; he remits his splendour, but retains his magnitude; and pleases more, though he dazzles less.[9] Economy, prudently and temperately conducted, is the safeguard of many virtues and is, in a particular manner, favourable to exertions of benevolence.[10]

The lovely young Lavinia once had friends,
And fortune smiled deceitful*² on her birth:
For, in her helpless years, deprived of all,
Of every stay, save* innocence and Heaven,
She, with her widow'd mother, feeble, old,
And poor, lived in a cottage, far retired
Among the windings of a woody vale;
By solitude and deep-surrounding shades,
But more by bashful modesty conceal'd.[11]

We find man? placed† in a world where he has by no means the disposal of the events that happen.[12] Attention was given that they should still have sufficient means† left to enable them to perform their military service.[13] Children often labour more to have the words in their books† imprinted on their memories, than to have the meaning† fixed in their minds.[14]

---

* *Save* may be considered a *preposition* here.—See K. No. 110.

† In many cases, the Infinitive *to be*, is understood before the Past Participle. Though the verb that follows *have*, *dare*, &c., is in the Infinitive, *to* is inadmissible, and where *to* is inadmissible, the *be* that follows it is inadmissible too.—Man *to be placed*—Means *to be left*, &c.—See Syn. R. 6.

EXERCISES IN PARSING.

Supply all the words that are understood. The infinitive *to be*, or *to have*, is often understood.—Not supplying what is understood after *than* and *as*, is frequently the cause of error.

No. p.

Disdain[a] even the appearance of falsehood, nor allow even the image of deceit a place in your mind.[1] Those[b] who want firmness and fortitude of mind seem born to enlist under a leader, and are the sinners or the saints of accident.[2] They lost their mother when very young.[3] Of all my pleasures and comforts, none have been so durable, satisfactory, and unalloyed, as those derived from religion.[4]

> For once upon a raw and gusty day,
> The troubled Tiber chafing with his shores,
> Cæsar says to me, " Dar'st thou, Cassius, now
> Leap[2d*] in with me into this angry flood,
> And swim to yonder point ?"[5]
>
> For contemplation he, and valour form'd:
> For softness she, and sweet attractive grace.[6]

Is not her younger sister fairer than she?[7] Only on the throne shall I be greater than thou.[8] We were earlier at church than they.[9] I have more to do than he.[10] He is as diligent as his brother.[11] I love you as well as him.[12] Virtue is of intrinsic value and good desert, and of indispensable obligation; not the creature of will, but necessary and immutable; not local or temporary, but of equal extent and antiquity with the divine mind; not a mode of sensation, but everlasting truth; not dependent on power, but the guide of all power.[13]

EXERCISES IN PARSING

1. The objective after an active verb, especially when a relative, is often understood.

2 Sometimes the antecedent is improperly omitted, and must be supplied.

No. q.

1. He that moderates his desires, enjoys the best happiness this world can afford.[1] Few reflections are more distressing than those we make on our own ingratitude.[2] The more true merit a man has, the more does he applaud it in others.[3] It is not easy to love those we do not esteem.[4] Our good or bad fortune depends on the choice we make of our friends.[5] An over-cautious attention to avoid evils often brings them upon us; and we frequently run headlong into misfortunes by the very means we pursue to avoid them.[6] He eats regularly, drinks moderately, and reads often.[7] She sees and hears distinctly, but she cannot write. Let him labour with his hands, that he may have to give to him that needeth.[9]

2. For reformation of error, there were that thought it a part of Christian duty to instruct them.[10] There have been that have delivered themselves from their misfortunes by their good conduct or virtue.[11]

  Who live to nature rarely can be poor,
  Who live to fancy rarely can be rich.[12]
  Who steals my purse steals trash.[13]

For if there be first a willing mind, it is accepted according to that a man hath, and not according to that he hath not.[14]

EXERCISES IN PARSING.

1. The objective generally comes *after* the verb that governs it; but when a *relative*, and in some other cases, it comes *before* it.
2. When two objectives follow a verb, the *thing* is governed by the *verb*, and the *person* by a *preposition* understood.

No. r.

1. Me ye have bereaved of my children.¹ Them that honour me I will honour.² Him whom ye ignorantly worship declare I unto you.³ Them that were entering in ye hindered.⁴ Me he restored to mine* office, and him he hanged.⁵ Those who have laboured to make us wise and good, are the persons whom we ought particularly to love and respect.⁶ The cultivation of taste is recommended by the happy effects which it naturally tends to produce on human life.⁷ These curiosities we have imported from China.⁸

2. And he gave him tithes of all.⁹ Who gave thee this authority?¹⁰ Ye gave me meat.¹¹ He gave them bread from heaven.¹² Give me understanding.¹³ Give me thine* heart.¹⁴ †Friend, lend me three loaves.¹⁵ Sell me thy birth-right.¹⁶ Sell me meat for money.¹⁷ I will send you corn.¹⁸ Tell me thy name.¹⁹ He taught me grammar.²⁰ If thy brother shall trespass against thee, go and tell him his fault between thee and him alone.²¹ Bring me a candle.²² Get him a pen.²³ Write him a letter.²⁴ Tell me nothing but the truth.²⁵

---

* *Mine*, a possessive pronoun, used here for *my*, as *thine* is for *thy*.
† *Friend* is the nominative, for he is *named*. Supply the ellipsis thus, *O thou who art my friend*, lend me, &c.

EXERCISES IN PARSING.

1. The poets often use an *adjective* as a *noun*; and sometimes join an *adjective* to their new-made noun.

2. They sometimes improperly use an *adjective* for an *adverb*.

3. Though the adjective generally comes *before* the noun, it is sometimes placed *after* it.

No. 5.

1. And where he *vital* breathes there must be joy
————— Who shall attempt with wandering feet
The dark, unbottomed, infinite abyss,
And through the *palpable* obscure find out
His uncouth way, or spread his airy flight,
Upborne with indefatigable wings,
Over the *vast* abrupt, e'er he arrive*
The happy isle?————*Paradise Lost*, b. ii. 404.

2. Thus Adam his illustrious guest besought:
And thus the god-like angel answered *mild*.[3]
The lovely young Lavinia once had friends,
And fortune smiled *deceitful* on her birth.[4]
When even at last the solemn hour shall come
To wing my mystic flight to future worlds,
I *cheerful* will obey; there, with new powers,
Will rising wonders sing.[5]
The rapid radiance *instantaneous* strikes
The illumin'd mountain.[6]————*Gradual* sinks the
Into a perfect calm.[7]   [breeze
Each animal, conscious of some danger, fled
Precipitate the loathed abode of man.[8]

3. But lose myself in him, in light *ineffable*.
————————— Pure serenity apace
Induces thought and contemplation *still*.[10]

---

* The poets often very improperly omit the preposition. It should be, "E'er he arrive *at* the happy isle." And again, "Here he had need all circumspection," for, need *of* all circumspection.

☞ After this, the Preface, with many other parts of the Grammar, may be used as additional exercises on Parsing.

A short explanation of some of the Terms used in the Grammar.

Nominative, naming
Possessive, possessing, belonging to.
Objective, the object upon which an active verb or preposition terminates.
Comparison, a comparing of qualities.
Positive, the quality without excess.
Comparative, a higher or lower degree of the quality.
Superlative, the highest or lowest degree of the quality.
Prefixing, placing before.
Personal, belonging to persons.
Relative, relating to another.
Antecedent, the word going before.
Demonstrative, pointing out.
Distributive, dividing into portions.
Indefinite, undefined, not limited.
Interrogative, asking.
Transitive, (action) passing to an object.
Intransitive, (action) confined to the actor; passing within.
Auxiliary, helping.
Conjugate, to give all the principal parts of a verb.
Mood, or *Mode*, form or manner of a verb.
Indicative, declaring, indicating.
Potential, having power, or will.
Subjunctive, joined to another under a condition.
Negative, no, denying.
Affirmative, yes, asserting.
Promiscuous, mixed.
Imperative, commanding.
Infinitive, without limits.
Tense, the time of acting or suffering.
Present, the time that now is.
Past, the time past.
Perfect, quite completed, finished, and past.
Pluperfect, more than perfect, quite finished some time ago.
Future, time to come.
Participle, partaking of other parts
Regular, according to rule.
Irregular, not according to rule.
Defective, wanting some of its parts.
Copulative, joining.
Disjunctive, disjoining.
Annexed, joined to.
Governs, acts upon.
Preceding, going before.
Intervene, to come between.
Unity, one—several acting as one.
Contingency, what may or may not happen; uncertainty.
Plurality, more than one.
Futurity, time to come.
Omit, to leave out, not to do.
Ellipsis, a leaving out of something.
Miscellaneous, mixed, of various kinds.
Cardinal,* principal, or fundamental.
Ordinal,† numbered in their order
Universal, extending to all.
Ambiguity, uncertainty which of the two it is.

---

* The *Cardinal numbers* are, One, two, three, four, five, six, seven, eight, nine, ten, &c.; from the first three are formed the adverbs *once, twice, thrice*.

† The *Ordinal numbers* are, First, second, third, fourth, fifth, sixth seventh, eighth, ninth, tenth, eleventh, twelfth, thirteenth, fourteenth, fifteenth, sixteenth, seventeenth, eighteenth, nineteenth twentieth, twenty-first, twenty-second, &c.

From these are formed *adverbs* of order; as, Firstly, secondly thirdly, fourthly, fifthly, sixthly, seventhly, eighthly, ninthly, tenthly, eleventhly, twelfthly, thirteenthly, fourteenthly, fifteenthly, sixteenthly, seventeenthly, eighteenthly, nineteenthly, twentiethly twenty-firstly, twenty-secondly, &c.

SYNTAX.

SYNTAX *is that part of Grammar which treats of the proper arrangement and connection of words in a sentence.**

A *sentence* is an assemblage of words making complete sense; as, *John is happy.*

Sentences are either simple or compound:

A *simple* sentence contains but one subject and one finite† verb; as, *Life is short.*

A *compound* sentence contains two or more simple sentences connected by one or more conjunctions; as, *Time is short,* BUT *eternity is long.*

A *phrase* is two or more words used to express a certain relation between ideas, without affirming anything; as, *In truth; To be plain with you.*

The principal parts of a simple sentence are, the *subject,* (or nominative,) the *attribute,* (or verb,) and the *object.*

The *subject* is the thing chiefly spoken of; the *attribute* is the thing affirmed or denied; and the *object* is the thing affected by such action.

---

* Syntax principally consists of two parts, *Concord* and *Government.* *Concord* is the agreement which one word has with another, in number, gender, case, or person.
 Government is that power which one part of speech has over another, in determining its mood, tense, or case.
† *Verbs* etc. are those to which number and person appertain. The *Infinitive* mood has no respect to number or person.

Rule I. *A verb must agree with its nominative in number and person;* as,—Thou readest, He reads; We read.

EXERCISES.

I loves reading. A soft* answer turn away wrath. We is but of yesterday and knowest nothing. Thou shall not follow a multitude to do evil. The days of man is but as grass All things is naked and open to the eyes of him with whom we has to do. All things was created by him. In him we live and moves. Frequent commission of crimes harden his heart. In our earliest youth the contagion of manners are observable. The pyramids of Egypt has stood more than three thousand years. The number of our days are with thee A judicious arrangement of studies facilitate improvement. A variety of pleasing objects charm the eye. A few pangs of conscience, now and then interrupts his pleasure, and whispers to him that he once had better thoughts. There is more cultivators of the earth than of their own hearts. Nothing but vain and foolish pursuits delight some persons. Not one of those whom thou sees clothed in purple are happy. There's two or three of us who have seen the work.

† Him and her were of the same age.

---

* Rule. *An adjective agrees with a noun in gender, number, and case* as, A *good* man.——As the *adjective*, in English, is not varied on account of *gender, number,* and *case,* this rule is of little importance.

† Rule. *The subject of a verb should be in the nominative:* thus, Him and her were married; should be, *He* and *she* were married.

☞ All those *Notes* at the bottom that have *Exercises* in the text are to be committed to memory and applied like the Rules at the top.

Rule II *An active verb governs the objective case;* as,—We love *him;* He loves *us.**

EXERCISES.

He loves we. He and they we know, but who art thou? She that is idle and mischievous, reprove sharply. Ye only have I known Let thou and I the battle try. He who committed the offence thou shouldst correct, not I who am innocent.

Esteeming theirselves wise, they became fools. Upon seeing I he turned pale. Having exposed hisself too much to the fire of the enemy, he soon lost an arm in the action.

The man whot he raised from obscurity is dead. Who did they entertain so freely? They are the persons who we ought to respect. Who having not seen we love. They who opulence has made proud, and who luxury has corrupted, are not happy.

‡ Repenting him of his design. It will be very difficult to agree his conduct with the principles he professes. Go, flee thee away into the land of Judea.

§ I shall premise with two or three general observations. He ingratiates with some by traducing others.

---

* The participle, being a part of the verb, governs the same case.

† Note. *When the objective is a relative, it comes before the verb that governs it.* (Mr. Murray's 6th rule is unnecessary.—See No. h, p. 65.)

‡ Rule I. *Neuter verbs do not admit of an objective after them:* thus, Repenting *him* of his design, should be, Repent ng ol his design.

§ Rule II. *Active verbs do not admit of a preposition after them.* Thus, I must premise *with* three circumstances, should be, I must premise three circumstances.

F

RULE. III. *Prepositions govern the objective case;* as —To *whom* much is given, of *him* much shall be required.

EXERCISES.

To who will you give that pen? Will you go with I? Without I ye can do nothing Withhold not good from they to who it is due. With who do you live? Great friendship subsists between he and I. He can do nothing of hisself. They willingly, and of theirselves, endeavoured to make up the difference. He laid the suspicion upon somebody, I know not who, in the company.

* Who do you speak to? Who did they ride with? Who dost thou serve under? Flattery can hurt none but those who it is agreeable to. It is not I thou art engaged with. It was not he that they were so angry with. Who didst thou receive that intelligence from? The person who I travelled with has sold the horse which he rode on during our journey. Does that boy know who he speaks to? I hope it is not I thou art displeased with.

† He is quite unacquainted with, and consequently cannot speak upon, that subject.

---

* Rule I. *The preposition should be placed immediately before the relative which it governs;* as, *To whom do you speak?*

The preposition is often separated from the relative; but though this is perhaps allowable in familiar conversation, yet, in solemn composition, the placing of the preposition immediately before the relative is more perspicuous and elegant.

† Rule II. *It is inelegant to connect two prepositions, or one and an active verb, with the same noun;* for example, They were refused entrance *into,* and forcibly driven *from,* the house; *should be,* They were refused entrance *into the house,* and forcibly driven *from it.*——I wrote to, and warned him; *should be,* I wrote to him and warned him.

RULE IV. *Two or more singular nouns coupled with* AND, *require a verb and pronoun in the plural;* as,—James *and* John *are* good boys; for *they* are busy.*

Two or more singular nouns separated by OR *or* NOR, *require a verb and pronoun in the singular;* as,—James *or* John *is* dux.†

EXERCISES.

Socrates and Plato was the most eminent philosophers of Greece. The rich and poor meets together. Life and death is in the power of the tongue. The time and place for the conference was agreed on. Idleness and ignorance is the parent of many vices. John and I reads better than you. Wisdom, virtue, happiness, dwells with the golden mediocrity. Luxurious living and high pleasures begets a languor and satiety that destroys all enjoyment. Out of the same mouth proceedeth blessing and cursing.

Neither precept nor discipline are so forcible as example. Either the boy or the girl were present. Neither character nor dialogue were yet understood. The modest virgin, the prudent wife, or the careful matron, are much more serviceable in life than petticoated philosophers. It must be confessed that a lampoon or a satire do not carry in them robbery or murder. Man is not such a machine as a clock or a watch which move merely as they are moved.

---

* *And* is the *only* conjunction that combines the agency of two or more into *one*; for, *as well as*, never does that; but merely states a sort of comparison; thus, "Cæsar, as well as Cicero, *was* eloquent."—*With* is sometimes used for *and.*—See *Miscellaneous Observations*, ⁋ 141 and 142.

† *Or* and *nor* are the only conjunctions appli— ⁋ this rule.

RULE V. *Conjunctions couple the same moods and tenses of verbs;* as,—*Do* good and *seek* peace

Conjunctions couple the same cases of nouns and pronouns; as,—*He* and *I* are happy.

EXERCISES.

He reads and wrote well. He or me must go. Neither he nor her can attend. Anger glances into the breast of a wise man, but will rest only in the bosom of fools. My brother and him are tolerable grammarians. The parliament addressed the king, and has been prorogued the same day. If he understands the subject, and attend to it, he can scarcely fail of success. Did he not tell thee his fault, and entreated* thee to forgive him? And dost thou open thine eyes upon such a one, and bringest* me into judgement with thee! You and us enjoy many privileges. Professing regard, and to act differently, mark a base mind. If a man have a hundred sheep, and one of them is gone astray, doth he not leave the ninety and nine, and goeth into the mountains, and seeketh that which is gone astray?

† Rank may confer influence, but will not necessarily produce virtue. She was proud, though now humble. He is not rich, but‡ is respectable. Our season of improvement is short; and, whether used or not,† will soon pass away

---

* The same *form* of the verb must be continued.

† Conjunctions frequently couple different moods and tenses of verbs; but in these instances the nominative is generally repeated, as, He *may return,* but he *will* not *continue.*

‡ The nominative is generally repeated, even to the same mood and tense, when a contrast is stated with *but, not,* or *though,* &c., as in this sentence.

ENGLISH SYNTAX

Rule VI. *One verb governs another in the infinitive mood;* as,—*Forget* not *to do good."*

To, *the sign of the infinitive, is not used after the verbs* bid, dare, need, make, see, hear, feel, let, perceive, behold, observe, have, *and* know.†

EXERCISES.

Strive learn. They obliged him do it. Newton did not wish obtrude his discoveries on the public. His penetration and diligence seemed vie with each other. Milton cannot be said have contrived the structure of an epic poem. Endeavouring persuade. We ought forgive injuries.

They need not to call upon her. I dare not to proceed so hastily. I have seen some young persons to conduct themselves very discreetly He bade me to go home. It is the difference of their conduct which makes us to approve the one, and to reject the other. We heard the thunder to roll. It is a great support to virtue, when we see a good mind to maintain its patience and tranquillity under injuries and afflictions, and to cordially forgive its oppressors. Let me to do that. I bid my servant to do this, and he doeth it. I need not to solicit him to do a kind office.

---

* The infinitive mood is frequently governed by *nouns* and *adjectives* as, They have a *desire* to learn; *Worthy* to be loved. *For,* before the infinitive, is unnecessary.

Let governs the objective case; as, Let *him* beware.

† *To* is generally used after the passive of these verbs, except *let* as. *He was made* to *believe it: He was let go;* and sometimes after the active, in the past tense, especially of *have,* a principal verb; as, I *had* to *walk* all the way.—See p. 61, *b.*

The *infinitive* is often independent of the rest of the sentence; as, *To proceed; To confess the truth,* I was in fault.

ENGLISH SYNTAX.

RULE VII. *When two nouns come together signifying different things, the first is put in the possessive case;* as,—John's book; on eagles' wings; his heart.

When two nouns come together signifying the *same* thing, they agree in case; as,—*Cicero* the *orator;* The city Edinburgh.

EXERCISES.

Pompeys pillar. Virtues reward. A mans manner's frequently influence his fortune. Asa his heart was perfect with the Lord. A mothers tenderness and a fathers care, are natures gifts for mans advantage. Helen her beauty was the cause of Troy its destruction. Wisdoms precepts are the good mans delight.

* Peter's, John's, and Andrew's occupation was that of fishermen. He asked his father is well as his mother's advice.

Jesus feet. Moses rod. Herodiast sake. Righteousness's sake. For conscience's sake. And they were all baptized of him in the river of Jordan.

---

* Rule. *When several nouns come together in the possessive case, the apostrophe with s is annexed to the last, and understood to the rest;* as, Jane and Lucy's books.

When *any words intervene, the sign of the possessive should be annexed to each;* as, This gained the *king's* as well as the *people's* approbation.

† To prevent too much of the hissing sound, the *s* after the apostrophe is generally omitted when the *first* noun has an *s* in each of its two *last* syllables, and the *second* noun begins with *s*; as, *Righteousness'* sake; *For conscience'* sake; *Francis'* sake.

It has lately become common, when the nominative singular ends in *s*, or *ss*, to form the possessive by omitting the *s* after the apostrophe; as, *James'* book, *Miss'* shoes, instead of *James's* book, *Miss's* shoes. This is improper. Put these phrases into *questions*, and then they will appear ridiculous. *Is this book James'?* *Are those shoes Miss'?* Nor are they less ridiculous without the interrogatory form; as, This book is *James'*, &c.—K. 195-6-7.

We sometimes use *of* instead of the *apostrophe* and *s*; thus we say, The *wisdom of* Socrates, rather than *Socrates's* wisdom. In some instances we use the *of* and the possessive termination too; as, It is a discovery *of* Sir Isaac *Newton's*, that is, one *of* Sir Isaac Newton's discoveries. A picture *of* my friend, means a *portrait of* him; but a picture of my *friend's*, means a portrait of some other person, and that it belongs to my friend.

Rule VIII. *When a noun of multitude conveys unity of idea, the verb and pronoun should be singular;* as,—The class *was* large.

When a noun of multitude conveys plurality *of idea, the verb and pronoun should be plural* as,—My people *do* not consider; *they* have no known me.

EXERCISES.

The meeting were well attended. The people has no opinion of its own. Send the multitude away, that it may go and buy itself bread. The people was very numerous. The council was not unanimous. The flock, and not the fleece, are, or ought to be, the object of the shepherd's care. When the nation complain, the rulers should listen to their voice. The regiment consist of a thousand men. The multitude eagerly pursues pleasure as its chief good. The parliament are dissolved. The fleet were seen sailing up the channel. Why do this generation seek after a sign? The shoal of herrings were immense. The remnant of the people were persecuted. The committee was divided in its sentiments. The army are marching to Cadiz. Some people is busy, and yet does very little. Never were any nation so infatuated. But this people who knoweth not the law are cursed.

As precise rules for the formation of the possessive case, in all situations, can scarcely be given, I shall merely subjoin a few *correct* examples for the pupil's imitation; thus, I left the parcel at *Smith's* the bookseller; The Lord Mayor of *London's* authority; For David thy *father's* sake; He took refuge at the *governor's* the *king's* representative; Whose glory did he emulate? He emulated *Cæsar's* the greatest general of antiquity. See *last note under* Rule XII, also Rule XXX.

RULE IX. *The verb* TO BE *should have the same case after it that it has before it;* as,—I am *he;* I took *it* to be *him.**

EXERCISES.

It was me who wrote the letter. Be not afraid, it is me. It was not me. It was him who got the first prize. I am sure it was not us that did it. It was them who gave us all this trouble. I would not act the same part again, if I were him. He so much resembled his brother, that at first sight I took it to be he. Search the Scriptures; for in them ye think ye have eternal life; and they are them which testify of me.

I saw one whom I took to be she. Let him be whom he may, I am not afraid of him. Who do you think him to be? Whom do men say that I am? She is the person who I understood it to have been. Whom think ye that I am? Was it me that said so? I am certain it was not him. I believe it to have been they. It might have been him. It is impossible to be them. It was either him or his brother that gained the first prize.

---

* When the verb *to be* is understood, it has the same case after it that it has before it ; as, He seems the leader of a party. I supposed him a man of learning : that is, *to be* the leader, &c., *to be* a man, &c

Part of a sentence is sometimes the nominative both before and after the verb *to be* ; as, His maxim was, " Be master of thy anger."

The verb *to be* is often followed by an *adjective.*—See No. III.

Passive verbs which signify naming, and some *neuter verbs*, have a nominative after them ; as, He shall be called *John* ; *He* became the *slave* of irregular passions. *Stephen* died a *martyr* for the Christian religion.

Some *passive* verbs admit an *objective* after them ; as, John was first denied *apples*, then he was promised *them*, then he was offered *them.*

Rule X. *Sentences that imply contingency and futurity require the Subjunctive Mood;* as,—*If he be alone, give him the letter.**

When contingency and futurity are not BOTH *implied, the Indicative ought to be used;* as,—*If he speaks as he thinks, he may safely be trusted.*

EXERCISES.

If a man smites his servant, and he die, he shall surely be put to death. If he acquires riches they will corrupt his mind. Though he be high, he hath respect to the lowly. If thou live virtuously, thou art happy. If thou be Christ, save thyself and us. If he does promise, he will certainly perform. Oh! that his heart was tender. As the governess were present, the children behaved properly. Though he falls he shall not be utterly cast down.

† Despise not any condition lest it happens to be thy own.* Let him that is sanguine, take heed lest he miscarries. Take care that thou breakest not any of the established rules.

‡ If he is but discreet, he will succeed. If he be but in health, I am content. If he does but intimate his desire, it will produce obedience.

---

* The exercises may all be corrected by the rule at the top.—K 201

† Rule I. *Lest and that annexed to a command require the Subjunctive Mood;* as, *Lest not sleep, lest thou come to poverty.* Take heed *that thou speak not to Jacob either good or bad.*

‡ Rule II. *If, with but following it, when futurity is denoted, requires the Subjunctive Mood;* as, *If he do but touch the hills they shall smoke.* But when future time is not expressed, the indicative ought to be used.

In the subjunctive the auxiliaries *shall, should, &c.,* are generally understood; as, Though he *fall*, i. e. though he *should* fall. Until repentance *compose* ten utters, i. e. until repentance *shall* compose See K 201.

ENGLISH SYNTAX.

RULE XI. *Some conjunctions have their correspondent conjunctions;* thus,—

Neither	requires	*Nor* after it; as, *Neither* he *nor* his brother was in
Though	Yet; as,	*Though* he was rich, *yet* for our sakes, &c.
Whether	Or	*Whether* he will do it *or* not, I cannot tell.
Either	Or*	*Either* she *or* her sister must go.
As	As	Mine is *as* good *as* yours.
As	So	*As* the stars *so* shall thy seed be. *As* the one dieth, *so* dieth the other.
Sot	As	He is not *so* wise *as* his brother. To see thy glo. v *so as* I have seen it, &c.
So	That	I am *so* weak *that* I cannot walk

EXERCISES.

It is neither cold or hot. It is so clear as I need not explain it. The relations are so uncertain, as that they require a great deal of examination. The one is equally deserving as the other. I must be so candid to own, that I have been mistaken. He would not do it himself, nor let me do it. He was as angry as he could not speak. So as thy days, so shall thy strength be. Though he slay me, so will I trust in him. He must go himself, or send his servant. There is no condition so secure as cannot admit of change. He is not as eminent, and as much esteemed, as he thinks himself to be. Neither despise the poor, or envy the rich, for the one dieth so as the other. As far as I am able to judge, the book is well written. His raiment was so white as snow

---

* The poets frequently use *Or—or*, for *Either—or*; and *Nor—nor* or *Neither—nor*.——In prose *not—nor* is often used for *neither—nor*.—The *yet* after *though* is frequently and properly suppressed.

Or does not require *either* before it when the one word is a mere explanation of the other..., or L. Sterling is enough.

† See K No. 204

ENGLISH SYNTAX 91

Rule XII. *When the present participle is used as a noun, it requires an article before it, and of after it;* as,—The sum of the moral law consists in *the obeying of* God, and *the loving of* our neighbour as ourselves.*

EXERCISES.

Learning of languages is very difficult. The learning any thing speedily requires great application. By the exercising our faculties they are improved. By observing of these rules you may avoid mistakes. By obtaining of wisdom thou wilt command esteem. This was a betraying the trust reposed in him. The not attending to this rule is the cause of a very common error.

† Our approving their bad conduct may encourage them to become worse. For his avoiding that precipice he is indebted to his friend's care.——‡ What is the reason of this person dismissing his servant so hastily? I remember it being done.

---

* These phrases would be right, were the *article* and *of both* omitted; as, The sum of the moral law consists in *obeying* God and *loving* our neighbour, &c. This manner of expression is, in many instances, preferable to the other. In some cases, however, these two modes express very different ideas, and therefore attention to the *sense* is necessary; as, He confessed the whole in *the hearing of* three witnesses, and the court spent an hour *in hearing* their deposition.—Key, No. 208.—&c.

† *The present participle with a possessive before it sometimes admits of* of *after it, and sometimes not;* as, Their observing *of* the rules prevented errors. By his studying the Scriptures he became wise.

When a preposition follows the participle, *of* is inadmissible; as, His depending on promises proved his ruin. His neglecting *to* study when young rendered him ignorant all his life.

‡ Rule. *A noun before the present participle is put in the possessive case;* as, Much will depend on the *pupil's composing* frequently.

Sometimes, however, the sense forbids it to be put in the possessive case; thus, What do you think of my *horse running* to-day? means, Do you think I should bet him run? but, What do you think of my *horse's running?* means, He has run, do you think he ran well?

ENGLISH SYNTAX.

RULE XIII. *The past participle is used after the verbs* have *and* be; as,—I have *written* a letter: he was *chosen.*

EXERCISES.

He has wrote his copy. I would have wrote a letter. He had mistook his true interest. The coat had no seam, but was wove throughout. The French language is spoke in every kingdom in Europe. His resolution was too strong to be shook by slight opposition. The horse was stole. They have chose the part of honour and virtue. The Rhine was froze over. She was showed into the drawing-room. My people have slid backwards. He has broke the bottle. Some fell by the wayside, and was trode down. The price of cloth has lately rose very much. The work was very well execute. His vices have weakened his mind, and broke his health. He would have went with us, had he been invited. Nothing but application is wanting to make you an excellent scholar.

* He soon begun to be weary of having nothing to do. He was greatly heated, and he drunk with avidity. The bending hermit here a prayer begun. And end with sorrows as they first begun.

A second deluge learning thus o'er-ran;
And the monks finished what the Goths began.

---

* Rule. The past participle must not be used instead of the past tense. It is improper to say he begun, for he began; he run, for he ran.

Rule XIV. *Pronouns agree in gender, number, and person, with the nouns for which they stand;* as,—John is here; *he* came an hour ago. Every tree is known by *its* fruit.

• EXERCISES.

Answer not a fool according to her folly. A stone is heavy, and the sand weighty; but a fool's wrath is heavier than it both. Can a woman forget his sucking child, that he should not have compassion on the son of her womb? yea, they may forget, yet will I not forget thee. Take handfuls of ashes of the furnace, and let Moses sprinkle it towards heaven, in the sight of Pharaoh; and it shall become small dust. Can any person, on their entrance into life, be fully secure that they shall not be deceived? The mind of man cannot be long without some food to nourish the activity of his thoughts.

* This boys are diligent. I have not seen him this ten days. You have been absent this two hours. Those sort of people fear nothing. We have lived here this many years. The chasm made by the earthquake was twenty foot broad, and one hundred fathom in depth. There is six foot water in the hold. I have no interests but that of truth and virtue. Those sort of favours did real injury.

---

* Rule. *Nouns* and *numeral adjectives must agree in number according to the sense;* thus, *This* boys, should be *these* boys, because boys is plural; and six *foot*, should be six *feet*, because *six* is plural.

Whole should never be joined to common nouns in the plural; thus Almost the *whole* inhabitants were present; should be, Almost *all* the inhabitants; but it may be joined to *collective* nouns in the plural, thus, *Whole* cities were swallowed up by the earthquake.

RULE XV. *The relative agrees with its antecedent in gender, number, and person;* as,—Thou *who* readest; The book *which* was lost

EXERCISES.

Those which seek Wisdom will certainly find her. This is the friend which I love. That is the vice whom I hate. This moon who rose last night. Blessed is the man which walketh in wisdom's ways. Thou who has been a witness of the fact, can give an account of it. The child which* was lost is found.

† The tiger is a beast of prey, who destroys without pity. Who of those men came to his assistance ?

‡ It is the best which can be got. Solomon was the wisest man whom ever the world saw It is the same picture which you saw before And all which beauty, all which wealth e'er gave, &c. The lady and lap-dog which we saw at the window. Some village Hampden. which, with dauntless breast, &c.

---

* It does not appear to me that it is harsh or improper, as Mr. Murray says, to apply *who* to *children*, because they have little reason and reflection ; but if it is, at what *age* should we lay aside *which* and apply *who* to them? *That* seems preferable to either. In our translation of the Bible, *who* and *that* are both applied to children, but never *which* See 2 Sam. xii, 14, 15. Matt. ii, 16. Rev. xii, 5.

† *Which* is applied to inferior animals, and also to persons in asking questions.

‡ Rule. THAT *is used instead of* WHO *or* WHICH :

1. *After adjectives in the* superlative degree,—*after the words* same *and* all, *and often after* some *and* any.

2. *When the antecedent consists of two nouns, the one requiring* who *and the other* which; as, The man and the horse *that* we saw yesterday

3. *After the interrogative* Who ; as,—Who *that* has any sense of religion would have argued thus ?

There seems to be no satisfactory reason for preferring *that* to *who* after *same* and *all*, except usage. The is indeed as good authority for using *who* after *all*, as for using *that* Johnson, for instance, uses *all who* several times in one paper

RULE XVI. *When the relative is preceded by two antecedents of* different persons, *it and the verb generally agree in person with the last;* as,—Thou art the *boy that was* dux yesterday.*

EXERCISES.

I am the man who command you. I am the person who adopt that sentiment, and maintains it. Thou art a pupil who possesses bright parts, but who hast cultivated them but little. I am a man who speak but seldom. Thou art the friend that hast often relieved me, and that has not deserted me now in the time of peculiar need. Thou art he who driedst up the Red Sea before thy people Israel.†

‡ The King dismissed his minister without any inquiry, who had never before committed so unjust an action. The soldier, with a single companion who passed for the bravest man in the regiment, offered his services.

---

* Sometimes the relative agrees with the former antecedent ; as, —I am verily a man who *am* a Jew. Acts xxii, 3.

The propriety of this rule has been called in question, because the relative should agree with the subject of the verb, whether the subject be next the relative or not. This is true, but it is also true that the subject is generally next the relative, and the rule is calculated to prevent the impropriety of changing from one person of the verb to another, as in the 3d example.

† When we address the Divine Being, it is, in my opinion, more direct and solemn to make the relative agree with the *second person*. In the Scriptures this is generally done. See Neh. ix, 7, &c. This sentence may therefore stand as it is.—In the third person singular of verbs, the solemn *eth* seems to become the dignity of the Almighty better than the familiar *es*; thus, I am the Lord thy God who *teacheth thee to profit*; who *leadeth* thee by the way that thou shouldst go; is more dignified than, I am the Lord thy God who *teaches* thee to profit, who *leads* thus.

‡ Rule. The relative ought to be placed next its antecedent, to prevent ambiguity: thus, The boy beat his companion, whom every body believed incapable of doing mischief; *should be*, The *boy, whom every body, believed incapable of doing mischief, beat his companion.*

ENGLISH SYNTAX.

Rule XVII. *When singular nominatives of different* persons *are separated by* or *or* nor *the verb agrees with the person next it ;* as,— Either thou or I *am* in fault: I, or thou, or he, *is* the author of it.*

EXERCISES.

Either I or thou am greatly mistaken. He or I is sure of this week's prize. Either Thomas or thou has spilt the ink on my paper. John or I has done it. He or thou is the person who must go to London on that business.

Promiscuous Exercises.

Your gold and silver is cankered. Fear and a snare is come upon us. The master taught him and I to read. Let not a widow be taken into the number under three-score years old, having been the wife of one husband, well reported of for good works; if she have brought up children, if she have lodged strangers, if she have washed the saints' feet, if she have relieved the afflicted, if she have diligently followed every good work. The candidate being chosen was owing to the influence of party. The winter has not been as severe as we expected it to be. Him and her were of the same age. If the night have gathered aught of evil, disperse it. My people doth not consider.

---

* The verb, though expressed only to the *last* person, is understood in its proper person to each of the rest, and the sentence when the ellipsis is supplied stands thus " Either thou *art* in fault, or I *am* in

ENGLISH SYNTAX

Rule XVIII. *A singular and a plural nominative separated by* OR *or* NOR, *require a verb in the plural;* as,—Neither the captain nor the sailors *were* saved.*

The plural nominative should be placed *next* the verb

EXERCISES.

Neither poverty nor riches was injurious to him. He or they was offended at it. Whether one or more was concerned in the business, does not yet appear. The cares of this life, or the deceitfulness of riches, has choked the seeds of virtue in many a promising mind. Neither the king nor his ministers deserves to be praised.

† A great cause of the low state of industry was the restraints put upon it. His meat were locusts and wild honey. His chief occupation and enjoyment were controversy.

‡ Thou and he shared it between them James and I are attentive to their studies. You and he are diligent in reading their books, therefore they are good boys.

---

sent and the next sentence. Either I *am* the author of it, or thou *art* the author of it, or he *is* the author of it.

Supplying the ellipsis thus would render the sentence correct; but so strong is our natural love of brevity, that such a tedious and formal attention to correctness would justly be reckoned stiff and pedantic. It is better to avoid both forms of expression when it can be conveniently done.

* The same observation may be made respecting the manner of supplying the ellipsis under this rule that was made respecting the last. A pardonable love of brevity is the cause of the ellipsis in both, and in a thousand other instances.

† Rule I. *When the verb* TO BE *stands between a singular and a plural nominative, it agrees with the one next it, or with the one which is more naturally the subject of it;* as, " The wages of sin is death."

‡ Rule II. *When a pronoun refers to two words of* different persons, *coupled with* and, *it becomes plural, and agrees with the first person when* I *or* we *is mentioned; and with the second, when* I *or* we *is not mentioned;* as, " John and I will lend you *our* books " " James and you have got *your* lessons."

RULE XIX. *It is improper to use both a noun and its pronoun as a nominative to the same verb* as,—*Man* that is born of a woman, *he* is of few days, and full of trouble ;—* omit *he*.

EXERCISES.

The king he is just. The men they were there. Many words they darken speech. My banks they are furnished with bees. Who, instead of going about doing good, they are perpetually intent upon doing mischief. Disappointments and afflictions, however disagreeable, they often improve us. Simple and innocent pleasures they alone are durable.

† Which rule, if it had been observed, a neighbouring prince would have wanted a great deal of that incense which has been offered up to him. ‡ Man, though he has great variety of thoughts, and such, from which others as well as himself might receive profit and delight, yet they are all within his own breast.

§ For he bringeth down them that dwell on high; the lofty city he layeth it low.

The friends thou hast, and their adoption tried,
Grapple them to thy soul with hooks of steel.

---

* In some cases where the noun is highly emphatical the repetition of it in the pronoun is not only allowable but even elegant : as The Lord *he* is the God. 1 Kings xviii, 39. See also Deut. xxi, 6.

† It ought to be, *If this rule had been observed*, a neighbouring, &c

‡ It ought to be, *Though man has* great variety, &c.

§ Rule. *It is improper to use both a noun and its pronoun as an objective after the same verb;* thus, in Deut. iv, 3. Your eyes have seen what the Lord did because of Baal-peor, for *all the men* that followed Baal-peor, the Lord thy God hath destroyed *them* from among you; *them* is superfluous, as a transposition of the last clause will show ; thus, For the Lord hath destroyed all the *men* from among you that followed Baal-peor

RULE XX. *The infinitive mood, or part of a sentence, is sometimes used as the nominative to a verb;* as,—For me *to live is* Christ, and *to die is* gain.* His being idle *was* the cause of his ruin.

EXERCISES.

To be carnally minded are death, but to be spiritually minded are life and peace. To live soberly, righteously, and piously, are required of all men. That warm climates should accelerate the growth of the human body, and shorten its duration, are very reasonable to believe. To be temperate in eating and drinking, to use exercise in the open air, and to preserve the mind from tumultuous emotions, is the best preservatives of health.

That it is our duty to promote the purity of our minds and bodies, to be just and kind to our fellow-creatures, and to be pious and faithful to Him who made us, admit not of any doubt in a rational and well-informed mind.

---

* The *infinitive* is equal to a noun; thus, *To play* is pleasant, and boys *love to play;* are equal to, *Play* is pleasant, and boy's love *play.*— p 64,h.

The *infinitive* is sometimes used instead of the present participle. *s*, To advise; To attempt; or *advising, attempting;* this substitution can be made only in the *beginning* of a sentence.

Note. Part of a sentence is often used as the *objective* after a verb: as, " You will soon find that the world does not perform what it promises." *What will you find? Ans.* That the world does not perform what it promises. Therefore, the clause, *that the world does not perform, &c.*, must be the objective after *find.* Did I not tell you thee that thou wouldst bring me to ruin? Here the clause, *that thou wouldst bring me to ruin* is the objective after *tell.*

RULE XXI. *Double comparatives and superlatives are inproper;* thus, Mine is a *more better* book, but John's is the *most best;* should be Mine is a *better* book, but John's is the *best*.

EXERCISES

The nightingale's voice is the most sweetest in the grove. James is a worser scholar than John. Tray is the most swiftest dog. Absalom was the most beautifulest man. He is the chiefest* among ten thousand.

His assertion was most untrue. His work is perfect; his brother's more perfect; and his father's the most perfect of all.

Promiscuous Exercises.

The great power and force of custom forms another argument against keeping bad company. And Joshua he shall go over before thee, as the Lord hath said. And God said, Let us make man in our image, after our likeness, and let them have dominion over the fish of the sea, &c. And the righteous men they shall judge them, &c. If thou be the King of the Jews, save thyself. The people, therefore, that was with him, when he raised Lazarus out of his grave, bare record. Public spirit is a more* universal principle than a sense of honour.

---

* *Chief, universal, perfect, true,* &c., imply the superlative degree without *est* or *most*. In language sublime or passionate, however, the word *perfect* requires the superlative form to give it effect. A lover enraptured with his mistress would naturally call her *the most perfect* of her sex.

Superior and *inferior* always imply comparison, and require *to* after them.

RULE XXII. *Two negatives in the same sentence are improper;** thus,—I *cannot* by *no* means allow it; *should be,* I *can* by *no* means allow it, *or,* I *cannot* by *any* means allow it.

EXERCISES.

I cannot drink no more. He cannot do nothing. We have not done nothing to-day. He will never be no taller. They could not travel no farther. Covet neither riches nor honours, nor no such perishing things. Nothing never affected her so much. Do not interrupt me thyself, nor let no one disturb me. I am resolved not to comply with the proposal, neither at present nor at any other time.

Promiscuous Exercises.

As far as I can judge, a spirit of independency and freedom, tempered by sentiments of decency and the love of order, influence, in a most remarkable manner, the minds of the subjects of this happy republic. James and I am cousins. Thy father's merits sets thee forth to view. That it is our duty to be pious admit not of any doubt. If he becomes very rich, he may be less industrious. It was wrote extempore. Romulus, which founded Rome, killed his brother Remus.

---

* Sometimes the two negatives are intended to be an affirmative as, *Nor* did they *not* perceive him; that is, they did perceive him. In this case they are proper.

When one of the negatives (such as *dis, in, un, im,* &c.) is joined to another word, the two negatives form a pleasing and delicate variety of expression; as, His language, though simple, is *not inelegant;* that is, it is *elegant.*

RULE XXIII. *Adverbs are, for the most part, placed before adjectives, after verbs active or neuter, and frequently between the auxiliary and the verb;* as,—He is *very* attentive: She behaves *well*, and is *much* esteemed.*

EXERCISES.

We should not be overcome totally by present events. He unaffectedly and forcibly spoke, and was heard attentively by the whole assembly. It cannot be impertinent or ridiculous, therefore, to remonstrate. Not only he found her employed, but pleased and tranquil also. In the proper disposition of adverbs, the ear carefully requires to be consulted as well as the sense.

† The women contributed all their rings and jewels voluntarily to assist the government. Having‡ not known, or having not considered, the measures proposed, he failed of success. He was determined to invite back the king, and to call together his friends.

§ Ask me never so much dowry.

* This is but a *general* rule. For it is impossible to give an exact and determinate one for the placing of adverbs on all occasions. The easy flow and perspicuity of the phrase ought to be chiefly regarded.

† The adverb is sometimes placed with propriety before the verb, or at some distance after it; as, The women *voluntarily contributed* all their rings and jewels, &c. They *carried* their proposition *farther*.

‡ *Not*, when it qualifies the present participle, comes *before* it.

§ *Never* is often improperly used for *ever*; thus, "If I make my hands *never* so clean." should be, "*ever* so clean."

☞ The note in former editions, stating that "*ly* is cut off from *exceedingly* when the next word ends in *ly*." has been removed, both because it properly belonged to the 24th Rule, and because it was in ome degree encouraging a breach of that rule. Two words which end in *ly* succeeding each other are indeed a little offensive to the ear, but rather than write bad grammar, it would be better either to offend it, or avoid the use of *exceedingly* in this case altogether; and instead of saying, "He need me *exceedingly discreetly*," say, "He used me *very discreetly*;" or, if that is not strong enough, vary the expression.

ENGLISH SYNTAX. 103

Rule XXIV. *Adjectives should not be used as adverbs, nor adverbs as adjectives;* as,—Remarkable well, for *remarkably* well; and, Use a little wine for thine often infirmities, instead of *thy frequent* infirmities; or,

Adverbs qualify adjectives and verbs—Adjectives qualify nouns.

EXERCISES.

They are miserable poor. They behaved the noblest. He fought bolder than his brother. He lived in a manner agreeably to the dictates of reason and religion. He was extreme prodigal, and his property is now near exhausted. They lived conformable to the rules of prudence. He speaks very fluent, reads excellent, but does not think very coherent. They came agreeable to their promise, and conducted themselves suitable to the occasion. They hoped for a soon and prosperous issue to the war.

* From whence come ye? He departed from thence into a desert place. Where† are you going? Bid him come here immediately. We walked there in an hour. He drew up a petition, where‡ he too frequently represented his own merit. He went to London last year, since when I have not seen him. The situation where I found him. It is not worth his while.

---

* Rule I. *From* should not be used before *hence, thence,* and *whence,* because it is *implied.*—In many cases, however, the omission of *from* would render the language intolerably stiff and disagreeable.

† Rule II. After verbs of motion, *hither, thither,* and *whither,* should be used, and not, *here, there,* and *where.*

‡ Rule III. *When* and *while* should not be used as nouns, nor *where* as a preposition and a relative; i. e. for *in which* &c.—For *while,* see Kay, 225.

Rule XXV. *The comparative degree, and the pronoun* other, *require* than *after them, and such* requires as; *as,—Greater* than *I,—No other* than *he ;—Such* as *do well.*

EXERCISES.

He has little more of the scholar besides the name. Be ready to succour such persons who need thy assistance. They had no sooner risen but they applied themselves to their studies. Those savage people seemed to have no other element but war. Such men that act treacherously ought to be avoided. He gained nothing farther by his speech, but only to be commended for his eloquence. This is none other but the gate of paradise. Such sharp replies that cost him his life. To trust in him is no more but to acknowledge his power.

† James is the wisest of the two. He is the weakest of the two. I understood him the best‡ of all others who spoke on the subject. Eve was the fairest of all her daughters. He is the likeliest of any other to succeed Jane is the wittier of the three, not the wiser

---

* Such, meaning either a *consequence*, or so great, requires *that ;* as His behaviour was *such, that* I ordered him to leave the room. Such is the influence of money, *that* few can resist it.

† Rule. *When two objects are compared, the comparative is generally used ; but when more than two, the superlative ;* as, This is the younger of the two ; Mary is the wisest of them all.

When the two objects form a *group*, or are not so much opposed to each other as to require *than* before the last, some respectable writers use the superlative, and say, " James is the *wisest* of the two." " He is the *weakest* of the two." The superlative is often more agreeable to the ear ; nor is the sense injured. In many cases a strict adherence to the comparative form renders the language too stiff and formal.

‡ A comparison in which *more* than two are concerned, may be expressed by the *comparative* as well as by the *superlative*, and in some cases better ; but the comparative considers the objects compared as belonging to *different* classes ; while the superlative compares them

Rule XXVI. *A pronoun after* than, *or* as, *either agrees with a verb, or is governed by a verb or preposition understood;* as,—He is wiser than I (am); She loved him more *than* (she loved) me.*

EXERCISES.

John can write better than me. He is as good as her. Thou art a much greater loser than me by his death. She suffers hourly more than me. They know how to write as well as him; but he is a better grammarian than them. The undertaking was much better executed by his brother than he. They are greater gainers than us. She is not so learned as him. If the king give us leave, we may perform the office as well as them that do.

† Who betrayed her companion? Not me. Who revealed the secrets he ought to have concealed? Not him; it was her. Whom did you meet? He. Who bought that book? Him. Whom did you see there? He and his sister. Whose pen is this? Mine's.

---

as included in *one* class. The comparative is used thus: "Greece was more polished than any other nation of antiquity." Here Greece stands by itself as opposed to the *other* nations of antiquity—She was none of the *other* nations—She was more polished than they. The same idea is expressed by the superlative when the word *other* is left out: Thus, "Greece was the most polished nation of antiquity." Here Greece is assigned the highest place in the class of objects *among which* she is numbered—the nations of antiquity—she is one of them

* When *who* immediately follows *than*, it is used improperly in the objective case: as, "Alfred, *than whom* a greater king never reigned:" —*than whom* is not grammatical. It ought to be. *than who*; because *who* is the noin to *was* understood—*Than whom* is as bad a phrase as, "He is taller *than him*." It is true that some of our best writers have used *than whom*: but it is also true, that they have used *other* phrases which we have rejected as ungrammatical: then why not reject this too?—The Exercises in the early editions of the Grammar have been *excluded*

† Rule The word containing the answer to a question, must be in the same case with the word which asks it: as, Who said that? I (said it.) Whose books are these? John's (books)

Rule XXVII. *The distributive pronouns,* each, every, either, neither, *agree with nouns and verbs in the singular number only;* as,— *Each* of his brothers *is* in a favourable situation; *Every* man is accountable for *himself*, *Either* of them *is* good enough.*

EXERCISES.

Let each esteem others better than themselves. Every one of the letters bear date after his banishment. Each of them, in their turn, receive the benefits to which they are entitled. Every person, whatever be their station, are bound by the duties of morality and religion. Neither of those men seem to have any idea that their opinions may be ill-founded. By discussing what relates to each particular in their order, we shall better understand the subject. Are either of these men your friend?

† And Jonathan, the son of Shimeah, slew a man of great stature, that had on every hand six fingers, and on every foot six toes.

‡ Nadab and Abihu, the sons of Aaron, took either of them his censer. The king of Israel and the king of Judah, sat either of them on his throne.

---

* *Each* relates to two or more objects, and signifies both of the two, or every one of any number taken singly.

† *Every* relates to *more* than *two* objects, and signifies each of them all taken individually.—It is quite correct to say, *Every six miles*.

Either signifies the *one* or the *other*, but *not both*. *Neither* imports *not either*.

‡ *Either* is sometimes improperly used instead of *each;* as, On *either* side of the river was there the tree of life: instead of, On *each* side of the river

ENGLISH SYNTAX. 107

Rule XXVIII. *When two persons or things are contrasted,* that *refers to the first mentioned, and* this *to the last*; as,—*Virtue* and *vice* are as opposite to each other as light and darkness, *that* ennobles the mind, *this* debases it.

EXERCISES.

Wealth and poverty are both temptations; this tends to excite pride, that discontentment. Religion raises men above themselves, irreligion sinks them beneath the brutes; that binds them down to a poor pitiable speck of perishable earth, this exalts them to the skies.

* And the cloud came between the camp of the Egyptians and the camp of Israel, and it was a cloud and darkness to them, but it gave light to these. Moses and Solomon were men of the highest renown; the latter was remarkable for his meekness, the former was renowned for his wisdom. I have always preferred cheerfulness to mirth; the former I consider as an act, the latter as a habit of the mind. Body and soul must part; the former wings its way to its almighty source, the latter drops into the dark and noisome grave.

---

* *Former* and *latter* are often used instead of *that* and *this*. They are alike in both numbers.

That and *this* are seldom applied to *persons*; but *former* and *latter* are applied to persons and things indiscriminately. In most cases however, the repetition of the noun is preferable to either of them

ENGLISH SYNTAX.

RULE XXIX. *In the use of verbs, and words that in point of time relate to each other, the order of time must be observed;* for example, I remember him these many years, should be, *I have remembered* him, &c.*

EXERCISES.

I have compassion on the multitude, because they continue with me now three days. And he that was dead sat up, and began to speak. The next new year's day I shall be at school three years. The court laid hold on all the opportunities which the weakness or necessities of princes afford it, to extend its authority. Ye will not come unto me that ye might have life. His sickness was so great, that I often feared he would have died before our arrival. It would have given me great satisfaction to relieve him from that distressed situation.

† I always intended to have rewarded my son according to his merit. We have done no more than it was our duty to have done From the little conversation I had with him, he appeared to have been a man of letters. It was a pleasure to have received his approbation of my labours. I intended to have written you last week.

---

* The best general rule that can be given, is, *To observe what the sense necessarily requires.*

† Rule. *After the Past Tense, the* present *infinitive (and not the* perfect) *should be used ;* as, I intended *to write* to my father, and not, I intended *to have* written ;—for however long it now is since I thought of writing, *to write* was then present to me, and must still be considered as present when I bring back that time, and the thoughts of it

Rule XXX. *It is improper to place a clause of a sentence between a possessive case and the word which usually follows it;* thus, She began to extol the farmer's, *as she called him,* excellent understanding; *should be,* She began to extol the excellent understanding of the farmer, as she called him.

EXERCISES.

They very justly condemned the prodigal's, as he was called, senseless and extravagant conduct. They implicitly obeyed the protector's, as they called him, imperious mandates. Beyond this, the arts cannot be traced of civil society. These are David's the king, priest, and prophet of the Jewish people's psalms. This is Paul's the Christian hero, and great apostle of the Gentile's advice.

* Howsoever beautiful they appear, they have no real merit. In whatsoever light we view him, his conduct will bear inspection. On whatsoever side they are contemplated, they appear to advantage. Howsoever much he might despise the maxims of the king's administration, he kept a total silence on that subject.

† Whoso keepeth the fig-tree shall eat the fruit thereof.

---

* Rule. Whichsoever *and* whatsoever, *are often divided by the interposition of the corresponding word;* thus, On whichsoever side the king cast his eyes; *should be,* On *which* side *soever* the king, &c.

I think this rule unnecessary, if not improper.—It would be better to say, *However* beautiful, &c. See my reasons, Key, p. 123. Nos 247—8—9.

‡ *Whoso* is an old word used instead of *he that;* as, Whoso mocketh the poor reproacheth his Maker; it should be, *He that* mocketh, &c

ENGLISH SYNTAX.

Rule XXXI. *Before names of places,*
To—is used after a verb of motion; as, We *went* to Spain.
At—is used after the verb *to be*; as, I *was* at Leith.
In—is used before names of countries and large cities: as, I live in London, *in* England.
At—is used before villages, towns, and foreign cities; as He resided *at* Gretna Green; *at* York; *at* Rome.

EXERCISES.

They have just arrived in Leith, and are going to Dublin. They will reside two months at England. I have been to London, after having resided at France; and I now live in Bath. I was in the place appointed long before any of the rest. We touched in Liverpool on our way for New-York. He resides in Mavisbank in Scotland. She has lodgings at George's Square.*

† Ah! unhappy thee, who are deaf to the calls of duty and of honour. Oh! happy‡ us, surrounded with so many blessings. Woe's I, for I am a man of unclean lips.

---

* One inhabitant of a city, speaking of another's residence, says, He stays in Bank-street; or if the word *number* be used, *at* No.—Prince's-street.—K. 195-6.

† Rule. The interjections *Oh!* and *Ah!* &c., generally require the *objective* case of the *first* personal pronoun, and the *nominative* of the *second*; as, Ah me! O thou fool! O ye hypocrites! Woe's *thou*, would be improper; it should be, Woe's *thee*; that is, Woe is *to thee*.

‡ *Interjections* sometimes require the objective case after them, but they never *govern* it. In the first edition of this Grammar, I followed Mr. Murray and others, in leaving *we*, in the exercises, to be turned into *us*; but that it should be *we*, and not *us*, is obvious; because it is the *Nom.* to *are* understood; thus, *Oh* happy *are we*, or, Oh *we are* happy (being) surrounded with so many blessings.

As interjections, owing to quick feelings, express only the *emotions* of the mind, without stopping to mention the *circumstances* that produced them; many of the phrases in which they occur are very elliptical, and therefore a verb or preposition must be understood. *Me*, for instance, in *Ah me*, is governed by *befallen* or *upon* understood: thus, *Ah*, what mischief has *befallen* me, or come *upon* me

Oh is used to express the emotion of *pain*, *sorrow*, or *surprise*.

O is used to express *wishing*, *exclamation*, or a direct *address* to a person.

ENGLISH SYNTAX 111

RULE XXXII. *Certain words and phrases must be followed with appropriate prepositions; such as*

Accused *of*—p. 131. b.
Abhorrence *of*
Acquit *of*
Adapted *to*
Agreeable *to*
Adverse *to*—see p. 113. b.
Bestow *upon*
Boast or brag *of**
Call *on* or *for*—p. 112. b.
Change *for*
Confide *in*†
Conformable *to*
Compliance *with*
Consonant *to*
Conversant *with, in*—p.113.b.
Dependent *upon*—p. 112. b.
Derogation *from*
Die *of* or *by*
Differ *from*
Difficulty *in*
Diminution *of*
Disappointed *in* or *of*—p.143.
Disapprove *of*‡
Discouragement *to*
Dissent *from*
Eager *in*
Engaged *in*

Exception *from*
Expert *at* or *in*
Fall *under*
Free *from*
Glad *of* or *at*—p. 113. b.
Independent *of* or *on*
Insist *upon*
Made *of*
Marry *to*
Martyr *for*
Need *of*
Observance *of*
Prejudice *against*
Profit *by*
Provide *with*
Reconcile *to*
Reduce *under* or *to*-p. 113
Regard *to*
Replete *with*
Resemblance *to*
Resolve *on*
Swerve *from*
Taste *for* or *of*—p. 150. b.
Think *of* or *on*—p. 112. b.
True *to*
Wait *on*
Worthy *of* §

---

* *Boast* is often used without *of*; as, For if I have *boasted* any thing.

† The same preposition that follows the *verb or adverb* generally follows the *noun* which is derived from it; as, Confide *in*, confidence *in*; disposed *to* tyrannize, a disposition *to* tyranny; independently *of*

‡ *Disapprove* and *approve* are frequently used without *of*.

§ *Of* is sometimes omitted, and sometimes inserted after *worthy*.

Many of these words take other prepositions after them to express other meanings; thus, for example, Fall *in*, to concur, to comply. Fall *off*, to forsake. Fall *out*, to happen. Fall *upon*, to attack. Fall *to*, to begin eagerly to eat; to apply himself *to*.

Exercises on Rule XXXII.

He was totally* dependent of the papal crown. He accused the minister for betraying the Dutch. You have bestowed your favours to the most deserving persons. His abhorrence to gaming was extreme. I differ with you. The English were very different then to what they are now. In compliance to his father's advice. He would not comply to his measures. It is no discouragement for the authors. The wisest princes need not think it any diminution to their greatness, or derogation to their sufficiency, to rely upon counsel. Is it consonant with our nature? Conformable with this plan. Agreeable with the sacred text. Call for your uncle.†

He was eager of recommending it. He had no regard after his father's commands. Thy prejudice to my cause. It is more than they thought‡ for. There is no need for it. Reconciling himself with the king. No resemblance with each other. Upon such occasions as fell into their cognizance. I am engaged with writing. We profit from experience. He swerved out of the path. He is resolved of going to the Persian court. Expert of his work. Expert on deceiving. The Romans

---

* *Dependent, dependence,* &c , are spelled indifferently with *a* or *e* in the last syllable.

† Call *for*—is to *demand,* to *require.* Call *on,* is to pay a short *visit* to *request ;* as, While you call *on* him—I shall call *for* a bottle of wine

‡ The authorities for *think of* and *think on* are nearly equal. The latter, however, abounds more in the Scriptures than the former, as, Think *on* me when it shall be well with thee : Think *upon* me for good : Whatsoever things are true, &c., think *on* these things. But *think of* is perhaps more common in modern publications.

Exercises on Rule XXXII.

reduced the world* to their own power. He provided them of every thing. We insist for it. He seems to have a taste of such studies. He died for thirst. He found none on whom he could safely confide. I dissent with the examiner. It was very well adapted for his capacity. He acquitted me from any imputation.' You are conversant† with that science. They boast in their great riches. Call of James to walk with you. When we have had a true taste for the pleasures of virtue, we can have no relish for those of vice. I will wait of you. He is glad of calamities.‡ She is glad at his company. A strict observance after times and fashions. This book is replete in errors. These are exceptions to the general rule. He died a martyr to Christianity. This change is to the better. His productions were scrupulously exact, and conformable with all the rules of correct writing. He died of the sword. She finds a difficulty of fixing her mind. This prince was naturally averse§ from war. A freeholder is bred with an aversion from subjection.

---

* Reduce *under*, is to subdue. In other cases, *to* follows it, as To reduce *to* practice, *to* fractions, &c.

† We say conversant *with* men *in* things. Addison has conversant *among* the writings of the most polite authors, and conversant *about* worldly affairs. Conversant *with* is preferable.

‡ *Glad of* is perhaps more proper, when the cause of joy is something gained or possessed; and *glad at*, when something befalls another; as, Jonah was exceedingly glad *of* the gourd; He that is glad *at* calamities, shall not be unpunished.

§ *Averse* and *aversion* require *to* after them rather than *from*; but both are used and sometimes even by the same author.

RULE XXXIII. All the parts of a sentence should correspond to each other, and a regular and dependent construction throughout be carefully preserved.* For example, the sentence, "He was more beloved, but not so much admired, as Cinthio," is inaccurate; because *more* requires *than* after it, which is no where found in the sentence. It *should be*, He was more beloved *than* Cinthio, but not so much admired.

A proper choice of words and a perspicuous arrangement should be carefully attended to.

EXERCISES.

The reward is his due, and it has[29] already, or will hereafter, be given to him. He was guided by interests always different,[32] sometimes contrary to those of the community. The intentions of some of these philosophers, nay of many, might[29] and probably were good. No person was ever so perplexed,[11] or sustained[25] the mortifications as he has done to-day. He was more bold and active,[25] but not so wise and studious as his companion. Then said they unto him, what shall we do that we might work[29] the works of God? Sincerity is as valuable,[11] and even more valuable,[26] than knowledge. The greatest masters of critical learning differ[32] among one another.

But from this dreary pēriod the recovery of the empire was become desperate; no wisdom could obviate its decādence. He was at one time thought to be a suppositious child.

---

* This rule is scarcely of any value as a rule: for every sentence on this page, except the last two, may be corrected by the preceding rules, as the reference by small figures will show; but it has been retained, because, where two words require a different construction, it will tend to correct the common error of forgetting the construction of the former word, and adhering to that of the latter.

ENGLISH SYNTAX

RULE XXXIV. *A* is used before nouns in the singular number only. *The** is used before nouns in both numbers.

The article is omitted before a noun that stands for a *whole species*; and before the names of minerals, metals, arts, &c.

The last of two nouns after a comparative should have no article when they both refer to *one* person; as, He is a better reader than writer.

To use the *Articles* properly is of the greatest importance; but it is impossible to give a rule applicable to every case.

Examples of the improper use and omission of the articles.

EXERCISES.

Reason was given to a man to control his passions. The gold is corrupting. A man is the noblest work of the creation. Wisest and best men are sometimes betrayed into errors. We must act our part with a constancy, though reward of our constancy be distant. There are some evils of life, which equally affect prince and people. Purity has its seat in the heart: but extends its influence over so much of outward conduct, as to form the great and material part of a character. At worst, I could but incur a gentle reprimand. The profligate man is seldom or never found to be the good husband, the good father, or the beneficent neighbour.

† He has been much censured for paying a little attention to his business. So bold a breach of order, called for little severity in punishing the offender.

---

* *The* is used before an *individual* representing the whole of its species, when compared with another individual representing another species; thus, *The* dog is a more grateful animal than *the* cat; i. e. *All* dogs are more grateful than cats.

† A nice distinction of the sense is sometimes made by the use or omission of the article *a*. If I say, He behaved with a little reverence; I praise him a little. If I say, He behaved with little reverence, I blame him.

116   ENGLISH SYNTAX.

Rule XXXV. An *ellipsis*, or *omission* of some words, is frequently admitted. Thus, instead of saying, He was a learned man, he was a wise man, and he was a good man; we say, He was a *learned, wise,* and *good* man.

EXERCISES.

A house and a garden. The laws of God, and the laws of man. Avarice and cunning may acquire an estate: but avarice and cunning cannot gain friends. His crimes had brought him into extreme distress, and extreme perplexity. He has an affectionate brother and an affectionate sister. By presumption, and by vanity, we provoke enmity, and we incur contempt. Genuine virtue supposes our benevolence to be strengthened and to be confirmed by principle. He is temperate, he is disinterested, he is benevolent. Perseverance in laudable pursuits, will reward all our toils, and will produce effects beyond our calculation. We often commend imprudently, as well as censure imprudently. Destitute of principle, he regarded neither his family nor his friends, nor his reputation. He insulted every man and every woman in the company. The temper of him who is always in the bustle of the world will be often ruffled and will be often disturbed.

* He regards his word, but thou dost not regard it. They must be punished, and they shall be punished. We succeeded, but they did not succeed.

---

* The auxiliaries of the compound tenses are often used alone, as We have done it, but thou hast not: *i. e.* thou hast not *done* it

ENGLISH SYNTAX. 117

Rule XXXVI. *An ellipsis is not allowable when it would obscure the sentence, weaken its force, or be attended with an impropriety;* for example, "We speak *that* we do know, and testify *that* we have seen," should be, We speak *that which* we do know, and testify *that which* we have seen.

EXERCISES.

*A noble spirit disdaineth the malice of fortune; his greatness of soul is not to be cast down. A house and† orchard. A horse and ass. A learned and amiable young man. I gladly shunned who gladly fled from me. A taste for useful knowledge will provide for us a great and noble entertainment when others leave us. They enjoy also a free constitution and laws. The captain had several men died in his ship of the scurvy. I must, however, be so candid to own I have been mistaken. The sacrifices of virtue will not only be rewarded hereafter, but recompensed even in this life. Oh, Piety! Virtue! how insensible have I been to thy charms! That is a property most men have, or at least may attain. There is nothing men are more deficient in, than knowing their own characters. Why do ye that which is not lawful to do on the sabbath days? Neither has he, nor any other persons, suspected so much dissimulation.

---

* A noble spirit disdaineth, &c., should be, *A man of a noble spirit disdaineth,* &c. This will render the sentence consistent with the rules of grammar and with common sense: to talk of the *soul* of a *spirit* is ridiculous.

† The article being once expressed, the repetition of it becomes unnecessary, except when a different form of it is requisite; as, A house and an orchard; and when some peculiar emphasis requires a repetition, as, Not only *the* year, but *the* day and *the* hour were appointed

CONSTRUCTION.

The four following lines are construed by way of example.—They were parsed at page 54. They are construed here, because the pupil should now be able to apply the Rules of Syntax.

> Oh how stupendous was the power
> That raised me with a word;
> And* every day and every hour,
> I lean upon the Lord.

How stupendous, adverbs are for the most part placed before adjectives, &c. *A power* is understood thus; *stupendous a power*,† an adjective agrees with a noun—*A power*, the article *a* is used before nouns in the singular number only—*the power*, *the* is used before nouns in *both* numbers—the *power was*, a verb agrees with its nominative—the *power that*, the relative agrees with its antecedent, &c. *That raised*, a verb agrees with its nom.—*Raised me*, an active verb governs the objective case—*With a word*, prepositions govern the objective—*A word*—*A* is used before nouns in the singular, &c. (*During* is understood) *during every day*, prepositions govern the objective case—*Every day*, an adjective agrees with a noun—*Day* and *hour*, conjunctions couple the same cases of nouns and pronouns; for *hour* is governed by *during* understood again—*Every hour*, an adjective agrees, &c.—*I lean*, a verb agrees with its nominative—*Upon the Lord*, prepositions govern the objective case.

The possessive pronouns, *My, Thy, His, Her, Our, Your, Their* and *Its*, must be construed exactly like nouns in the *possessive case* for a pronoun is an exact resemblance of a noun in *every* thing but *one*; namely, it will not admit of an *adjective* before it like a noun. *His* is equal to *John's*, and *her* to *Ann's*, and *their* to the *men's*, in the following sentences.

John lost *his* gloves, i. e. John lost *John's* gloves.—Ann found *her* book, i. e. Ann found *Ann's* book. The men took off *their* hats, i. e. The men took off the *men's* hats. The garden is productive, and *its* fruit is good, i. e. the *garden's* fruit. In all these cases, and in such phrases as, *my* house—*thy* field—*our* lands—*your* estates—*their* property—*whose* horse,—the rule is, " When two nouns come together, signifying different things, the first is put in the possessive case."

---

* It is impossible to construe bad grammar. *And* here is so very vaguely used, that the rule, "Conjunctions couple the same moods and tenses of verbs, and the same cases of nouns and pronouns," will not apply in this passage. From the sense, it is evident that *And* should be *Yea*, meaning *not only so, but*—every day, &c.

† Or, how stupendous *the power was*, but it is certainly better to supply *a power* thus; O how stupendous *a power* was the power that raised me with a word.

PROMISCUOUS EXERCISES.

On the Rules of Syntax.

John writes pretty. Come here, James. Where are you going, Thomas? I shall never do so no more. The train of our ideas are often interrupted. Was you present at last meeting? He need not be in so much haste. He dare not act otherwise than he does. Him whom they seek is in the house. George or I is the person. They or he is much to be blamed. The troop consist of fifty men. Those set of books was a valuable present. A pillar sixty foot high. His conduct evinced the most extreme vanity. These trees are remarkable tall. He acted bolder than was expected. This is he who I gave the book to. Eliza always appears amiably. She goes there to-morrow. From whence came they? Who do you lodge with now? He was born at London, but he died in Bath. If he be sincere I am satisfied. Her father and her were at church. The master requested him and I to read more distinctly. It is no more but his due. Flatterers flatter as long, and no longer than they have expectations of gain. John told the same story as you told. This is the biggest one which I have ever seen.

PROMISCUOUS EXERCISES.

Let he and I read the next chapter. She is free of pain. Those sort of dealings are unjust. David the son of Jesse was the youngest of his brothers. You was very kind to him, he said. Well, says I, what does thou think of him now? James is one of those boys that was kept in at school, for bad behaviour. Then, James, did deny the deed. Neither good nor evil come of themselves. We need not to be afraid. He expected to have gained more by the bargain. You should drink plenty of goat milk. It was him who spoke first. Do you like ass milk? Is it me that you mean? Who did you buy your grammar from? If one takes a wrong method at first setting out, it will lead them astray. Neither man nor woman were present. I am more taller than you. She is the same lady who sang so sweetly. After the most straitest sect of our religion, I lived a Pharisee. Is not thy wickedness great? and thine iniquities infinite? There was more sophists than one. If a person have lived twenty or thirty years, he should have some experience. If this were his meaning, the prediction has failed. Fidelity and truth is the foundation of all justice. His associates in wickedness will not fail to mark the alteration of his conduct. Thy rod and thy staff they comfort me.

PROMISCUOUS EXERCISES.

And when they had lift up their eyes, they saw no man save Jesus only. Strive not with a man without cause, if he have done thee no harm. I wrote to, and cautioned the captain against it. Now both the chief priests and Pharisees had given a commandment, that if any man knew where he were, he should show it, that they might take him. The girl her book is torn in pieces. It is not me who he is in love with. He which commands himself, commands the whole world. Nothing is more lovelier than virtue.

The peoples happiness is the statesmans honour. Changed to a worser shape thou canst not be. I have drunk no spiritnous liquors this six years. He is taller than me, but I am stronger than him. Solid peace and contentment consists neither in beauty or riches, but in the favour of God. After who is the King of Israel come out? The reciprocations of love and friendship between he and I, have been many and sincere. Abuse of mercies ripen us for judgment. Peter and John is not at school to-day. Three of them was taken into custody. To study diligently, and behave genteelly, is commendable. The enemies who we have most to fear are those of our own hearts. Regulus was reckoned the most consummate warrior that Rome could then produce. Suppose life never so long, fresh accessions of knowledge may still be made

PROMISCUOUS EXERCISES.

Surely thou who reads so much in the Bible, can tell me what became of Elijah Neither the master nor the scholars is reading. Trust not him, whom, you know, is dishonest. I love no interests but that of truth and virtue. Every imagination of the thoughts of the heart are evil continually. No one can be blamed for taking due care of their health. They crucified him, and two others with him, on either side one, and Jesus in the midst.

I have read Popes Homer, and Drydens Virgil. He that is diligent you should commend. There was an earthquake which made the earth to tremble. And God said to Solomon, Wisdom and knowledge is granted unto thee, &c. I cannot commend him for justifying hisself when he knows that his conduct was so very improper. He was very much made on at school. Though he were a son, yet learned he obedience by the things which he suffered. If he is alone tell him the news; but if there is any body with him, do not tell him. They ride faster than us. Though the measure be mysterious, it is worthy of attention. If he does but approve my endeavours, it will be an ample reward. Was it him who came last? Yes, it was him.

> For ever in this humble cell,
> Let thee and I my fair one dwell

PROMISCUOUS EXERCISES.

Every man should act suitable to his character and station in life. His arguments were exceeding clear. I only spoke three words on that subject. The ant and the bee sets a good example before dronish boys. Neither in this world, neither in the world to come. Evil communications corrupts good manners. Hannibal was one of the greatest generals whom the world ever saw. The middle station of life seems to be the most advantageously situated for gaining of wisdom.

These are the rules of grammar, by the observing which you may avoid mistakes. The king conferred on him the title of a duke. My exercises are not well wrote, I do not hold my pen well. Grammar teaches us to speak proper. She accused her companion for having betrayed her. I will not dissent with her Nothing shall make me swerve out of the path of duty and honour. Who shall I give it to? Who are you looking for? It is a diminution to, or a derogation of their judgement. It fell into their notice or cognizance. She values herself for her fortune. That is a book which I am much pleased with. I have been to see the coronation, and a fine sight it was. That picture of the emperor's is a very exact resemblance of him. Every thing that we here enjoy, change, decay, and come to an end. It is not him they blame so much.

PROMISCUOUS EXERCISES.

No people has more faults than they that pretend to have none. The laws of Draco is said to have been wrote with blood. It is so clear, or so obvious, as I need not explain it. She taught him and I to read. The more greater a bad man's accomplishments are, the more dangerous he is to society, and the more less fit for a companion. Each has their own faults, and every one should endeavour to correct their own. Let your promises be few, and such that you can perform.

His being at enmity with Cæsar and Antony were the cause of perpetual discord. Their being forced to their books in an age at enmity with all restraint, have been the reason why many have hated books all their lives. There was a coffee-house at that end of the town, in which several gentlemen used to meet of an evening. Do not despise the state of the poor, lest it becomes your own condition. It was his duty to have interposed his authority in an affair of so much importance. He spent his whole life in the doing good. Every gentleman who frequented the house, and conversed with the erectors of this occasional club, were invited to pass an evening when they thought fit. The winter has not been so severe as we expected it to have been. The rest (of the stars) in circuit walls this universe: Sir, if thou have borne him hence, tell me where thou hast laid him.

PROMISCUOUS EXERCISES.

A lampoon, or a satire, does not carry in it either robbery or murder. She and you were not mistaken in her conjectures. My sister and I, as well as my brother, are employed in their respective occupations. He repents him of that indiscreet action. It was me, and not him, that wrote it. Art thou him? I shall take care that no one shall suffer no injury. I am a man who approves of wholesome discipline, and who recommend it to others; but I am not a person who promotes severity, or who object to mild and generous treatment This Jackanapes has hit me in a right place enough. Prosperity, as truly asserted by Seneca, it very much obstructs the knowledge of ourselves. To do to others as we would that they should do to us, it is our duty. This grammar was purchased at Ogle's the bookseller's. The council was not unanimous.

Who spilt the ink upon the table? Him. Who lost this book? Me. Whose pen is this? Johns. There is in fact no impersonal verbs in any language. And he spitted on the ground, and anointed his eyes. Had I never seen ye, I had never known ye. The ship Mary and Ann were restored to their owners If we consult the improvement of mind, or the health of body, it is well known exercise is the great instrument for promoting both. A man may see a metaphor or an allegory in a picture, as well as read them in a description.

PROMISCUOUS EXERCISES

I had no sooner placed her at my right hand, by the fire, but she opened to me the reason of her visit. A prudent wife, she shall be blessed. The house you speak of, it cost me five hundred pounds. Did I not tell thee, O thee infamous wretch! that thou wouldst bring me to ruin? Not only the counsel's and attorney's, but the judge's opinion also favoured his cause. It was the men's, women's, and children's lot, to suffer great calamities. That is the eldest son of the King of England's. Lord Feversham the general's tent. This palace had been the grand Sultan's Mahomet's. They did not every man cast away the abomination of their eyes.

* I am purposed. He is arrived. They were deserted from their regiment. Whose works are these? They are Cicero, the most eloquent of men's. The mighty rivals are now at length agreed. The time of William making the experiment, at length arrived. If we alter the situation of any of the words, we shall presently be sensible of the melody suffering. This picture of the king's does not much resemble him. These pictures of the king were sent to him from Italy. He who committed the offence, thou should'st correct not I, who am innocent.

---

* Rule. It is improper to use a neuter verb in the passive form. Thus I am purposed—He is arrived — should be, I have purposed—He has arrived.——From this rule there are a number of exceptions; & it is allowable to say, He is come. She is gone &c.

PROMISCUOUS EXERCISES.

But Thomas, one of the twelve, called Didymus, was not with them when Jesus came I offer observations, that a long and chequered pilgrimage have enabled me to make on man. After I visited Europe, I returned to America. Clelia is a vain woman, whom, if we do not flatter, she will be disgusted. In his conduct was treachery, and in his words faithless professions. The orators did not forget to enlarge themselves on so popular a subject. He acted conformable with his instructions, and cannot be censured justly.

No person could speak stronger on this subject, nor behave nobler, than our young advocate, for the cause of toleration. They were studious to ingratiate with those who it was dishonourable to favour. The house framed a remonstrance, where they spoke with great freedom of the king's prerogative. Neither flatter or contemn the rich or the great. Many would exchange gladly their honours, beauty, and riches, for that more quiet and humbler station, which thou art now dissatisfied with. High hopes, and florid views, is a great enemy to tranquillity. Many persons will not believe but what they are free from prejudices. I will lay me down in peace, and take my rest. This word I have only found in Spenser. The king being apprized of the conspiracy, he fled from Jerusalem.

PROMISCUOUS EXERCISES.

A too great variety of studies dissipate and weaken the mind. James was resolved to not indulge himself in such a cruel amusement. They admired the countryman's, as they called him, candour and uprightness. The pleasure or pain of one passion differ from those of another. The court of Spain, who gave the order, were not aware of the consequences. There was much spoke and wrote on each side of the question; but I have chose to suspend my decision.

Religion raises men above themselves; irreligion sinks them beneath the brutes; that binds them down to a poor pitiable speck of perishable earth; this opens for them a prospect to the skies. Temperance and exercise, howsoever little they may be regarded, they are the best means of preserving health. To despise others on account of their poverty, or to value ourselves for our wealth, are dispositions highly culpable. This task was the easier performed, from the cheerfulness with which he engaged in it. These counsels were the dictates of virtue, and the dictates of true honour. As his misfortunes were the fruit of his own obstinacy, a few persons pitied him And they were judged every man according to their works. Riches is the bane of human happiness. I wrote to my brother before I received his letter.

PROMISCUOUS EXERCISES.

When Garrick appeared, Peter was for some time in doubt whether it could be him or not. Are you living contented in spirit and darkness? The company was very numerous. Shall the throne of iniquity have fellowship with thee, which frameth mischief by a law? Where is the security that evil habits will be ever broken? They each bring materials to the place. Nor let no comforter delight my ear. She was six years older than him. They were obliged to contribute more than us. The Barons had little more to rely on, besides the power of their families. The sewers (shores) must be kept so clear, as the water may run away. Such among us who follow that profession. No body is so sanguine to hope for it. She behaved unkinder than I expected. Agreeable to your request I send this letter. She is exceeding fair. Thomas is not as docile as his sister. There was no other book but this. He died by a fever. Among whom was Mary Magdalene, and Mary the mother of James. My sister and I waited till they were called. The army were drawn up in haste. The public is respectfully informed, that, &c. The friends and amusements which he preferred corrupted his morals. Each must answer for themselves. Henry, though at first he showed an unwillingness, yet afterwards he granted his request.

1

PROMISCUOUS EXERCISES.

Him and her live very happily together She invited Jane and I to see her new dress She uttered such cries that pierced the heart of every one who heard them. Maria is not as clever as her sister Ann. Though he promises ever so solemnly, I will not believe him. The full moon was no sooner up, in all its brightness, but he opened to them the gate of paradise. It rendered the progress very slow of the new invention. This book is Thomas', that is James'. Socrates's wisdom has been the subject of many a conversation. Fare thee well, James. Who, who has the judgement of a man, would have drawn such an inference? George was the most diligent scholar whom I ever knew. I have observed some children to use deceit. He durst not to displease his master. The hopeless delinquents might, each in their turn adopt the expostulatory language of Job Several of our English words, some centuries ago, had different meanings to those they have now. And I was afraid, and went and hid thy talent in the earth; lo, there thou hast that is thine. With this booty, he made off to a distant part of the country, where he had reason to believe that neither he nor his master were known Thine is the kingdom, the power, and the glory I have been at London.

PROMISCUOUS EXERCISES.

Which of the two masters, says Sĕneca shall we most esteem? He who strives to correct his scholars by prudent advice and motives of honour, or another who will lash them severely for not repeating their lessons as they ought! The blessing of the Lord it maketh rich, and he addeth no sorrow with it. For if there be first a willing mind, it is accepted according to that a man hath, and not according to that he hath not. If a brother or a sister be naked and destitute of daily food, and one of you say unto them, Depart in peace, be ye warmed and filled; notwithstanding if ye give them not those things which are needful to the body, what doth it profit?

But she always behaved with great severity to her maids; and if any of them were negligent of their duty, or made a slip in their conduct, nothing would serve her but burying the poor girls alive. He had no master to instruct him; he had read nothing but the writings of Moses and the prophets, and had received no lessons from the Socrates's,* the Plato's, and the Confucius's of the age. They that honour me, I will honour. For the poor always ye have with you.

---

* The *Possessive case* must not be used for the *plural* number. In this quotation from Baron Haller's Letters to his Daughter, the proper names should have been pluralized like common nouns; thus, From two *Socrateses*, the *Platoes*, and the *Confuciuses* of the age.

PROMISCUOUS EXERCISES.

The first Christians of the gentile world made a simple and entire transition from a state as bad, if not worse, than that of entire ignorance, to the Christianity of the New Testament.

And he said unto Gideon, every one that lappeth of the water with his tongue, as a dog lappeth, him shalt thou set by himself.

The duke had not behaved with that loyalty as was expected.

Milton seems to have been well acquainted with his own genius, and to know what it was that nature had bestowed upon him more bountifully than upon others.

And on the morrow, because he would have known the certainty wherefore he was accused* by the Jews, he loosed him from his bonds.

  Here rages force, here tremble flight and fear,
  Here stormed contention, and here fury frowned.

  The Cretan javelin reached him from afar,
  And pierced his shoulder as he mounts his car.

Nor is it then a welcome guest, affording only an uneasy sensation, and brings always with it a mixture of concern and compassion.

He only† promised me a loan of the book for two days. I was once thinking to have written a poem.

---

* *Accuse* requires *of* before the *crime*, and *by* before the *person accusing*.

† This sentence expresses one meaning as it stands. It may be made to express other four by placing *only* after *me*, or *loan*, or *book*, or *days*.

PROMISCUOUS EXERCISES.

A very slow child will often be found to get lessons by heart as soon as, nay sometimes sooner, than one who is ten times as intelligent.

It is then from a cultivation of the perceptive faculties, that we only can attain those powers of conception which are essential to taste.

No man is fit for free conversation for the inquiry after truth, if he be exceedingly reserved; if he be haughty and proud of his knowledge; if he be positive and dogmatical in his opinions: if he be one who always affects to outshine all the company; if he be fretful and peevish; if he affect wit, and is full of puns, or quirks, or quibbles.

Conversation is the business, and let every one that please add their opinion freely.

> The mean suspicious wretch whose bolted door
> Ne'er moved in duty to the wandering poor;
> With him I left the cup, to teach his mind,
> That heaven can bless if mortals will be kind.

There are many more shining qualities in the mind of man, but there is none so useful as discretion.

Mr. Locke having been introduced by Lord Shaftesbury to the Duke of Buckingham and Lord Halifax, these three noblemen, instead of conversing with the philosopher on literary subjects, in a very short time sat down to cards.

PROMISCUOUS EXERCISES.

Bad Arrangement.

It is your light fantastic fools, who have neither heads nor hearts, in both sexes, who, by dressing their bodies out of all shape, render themselves ridiculous and contemptible.

And how can brethren hope to partake of their parent's blessing that curse each other.

The superiority of others over us, though in trivial concerns, never fails to mortify our vanity, and give us vexation, as Nicole admirably observes.

Likewise also the chief priests, mocking said among themselves, with the scribes, He saved others; himself he cannot save.

Noah, for his godliness, and his family were the only persons preserved from the flood.

It is an unanswerable argument of a very refined age, the wonderful civilities that have passed between the nation of authors, and that of readers.

And they said among themselves, who shall roll us away the stone from the door of the sepulchre? And when they had looked, they saw that the stone was rolled away: for it was very great.

A great stone that I happened to find, after a long search, by the sea-shore, served me for an anchor.

It is true what he says, but it is not applicable to the point.

PROMISCUOUS EXERCISES

Bad Arrangement *

The senate of Rome ordered that no part of it should be rebuilt; it was demolished to the ground, so that travellers are unable to say where Carthage stood at this day.

Thus ended the war with Antiochus, twelve years after the second Punic war, and two after it had been begun.

Upon the death of Claudius, the young Emperor, Nero, pronounced his funeral oration and he was canonized among the gods, who scarcely deserved the name of a man.

Galerius abated much of his severities against the Christians on his death-bed, and revoked those edicts which he had formerly published, tending to their persecution, a little before his death.

The first care of Aurelius was to marry his daughter Lucilla once more to Claudius Pompeianus, a man of moderate fortune, &c.

But at length, having made his guards accomplices in their design, they set upon Maximin while he slept at noon in his tent, and slew both him and his son, whom he had made his partner in the empire, without any opposition.

Aurelian defeated the Marcomanni, a fierce and terrible nation of Germany, that had invaded Italy, in three several engagements.

---

* The exercises on this page are all extracted from the octavo edition of Goldsmith's Roman History, from which many more might be got. It is amazing how many mistakes even our most popular authors have made.

AMBIGUITY.

You suppose him younger than I.

This may mean, either that you suppose him younger than I am, or that you suppose him to be younger than I suppose him to be.

Parmēnio had served with great fidelity, Philip, the father of Alexander, as well as himself, for whom he first opened the way into Asia.

Here we are apt to suppose the word *himself* refers to Parmēnio, and means that he had not only served *Philip*, but he had served himself at the same time. This however is not the meaning of the passage. If we arrange it thus, the meaning will appear. "Parmēnio had not only served Philip the father of Alexander with great fidelity, but he had served *Alexander himself*, and was the first that opened the way for him into Asia."

Belisarius was general of all the forces under the emperor Justinian the First, a man of rare valour.

Who was a man of rare valour? The *emperor Justinian* we should suppose, from the arrangement of the words; but this is not the case, for it was *Belisarius*. The sentence should have stood thus, "Belisarius, a man of rare valour was general of all the forces under the emperor Justinian the First."

Lisias promised to his father never to abandon his friends.

Whether were they his own friends or his *father's* whom Lisias promised never to abandon? If his *own*, it should be, Lisias promised and said to his father, I will never abandon *my friends*. If his *father's*, it should be, Lisias promised and said to his father, I will never abandon *your friends*.

IMPROPER EXPRESSIONS.

Tautology, or the repetition of a thought or word already fully expressed, is improper.

EXAMPLES.

The *latter end* of * man shall be peace
Whenever I try to improve, I *always* find I can do it.
I saw it *in here*—I saw it *here*.
He was *in here* yesterday when I spoke to him.
Give me both of these books.—Give me *both those* books.
They *both* met—They met.
I never fail to read, when ever I can get a book—*when*.
You must return *t* back immediately.
First of all I shall say my lesson *last of all* I will say, &c.
If *ever* I do it, I must *t* do it fresh.
He plunged *t* down into the water.
Read from *here* to *there*—from *this* to *that*.
Take up your book, and read it *attentively* over again.
This was the *sickest* accident *of all others*.
I ran after him a little way, but he returned *t back t again*.
I cannot tell *t for why* he did it.
Learn *t from hence* to study the Scriptures diligently.
Where shall I set out *t from* was not said.
We must do it as fast *t* as *t* we can. I will *t* see *t therefore*, I say.
I found nobody *t else but t him* at home.
Such ascends *t up* into the clouds.
We hastily *descended t down from* the mountain.
He raised *t up* his arm to strike me.
We were *t mutually* friendly to each other.
It should *t ever* be your constant study to do good.
As soon as I awoke I rose *t up* and dressed myself.
I leave town in the *t latter end* of July.

☞ *Avoid the following vulgar phrases:*—Behoof, behest, fell to work, wherewithal, quoth he, do away, long winded, chalked out, pop out, must needs, got rid of, handed down, self-same, pell mell, that's your sort, tip him the wink, pitched upon.——*Subject matter* is a detestable phrase.——*Subject*.

---

* The word immediately after the dagger is to be omitted, because it is superfluous.
* *These*, if the person has them in his hand.

IMPROPER EXPRESSIONS.

My every hope, *should be*	*All my* hopes.
Frequent opportunity.	Frequent *opportunities*.
Who finds him in money?	Who finds him *money*?
He put it in his pocket.	He put it *into* his pocket.
No less than fifty persons.	No *fewer* than fifty persons.
The two first steps are new	The *first two* steps are new
All over the country.	*Over all* the country.
Be that as it will.	Be that as it *may*.
About two years back.	About two years *ago*.
He was to come as this day.	He was to come this day.
They retreated back.	They retreated.
't lays on the table.	It *lies* on the table.
I turned them topsy turvy.	I *overset* them.
I catch'd it.	I *caught* it.
How does thee do?	How *dost thou* do?
Overseer over his house.	Overseer *of* his house.
Opposite the church.	Opposite *to* the church.
Provisions were plenty.	Provisions were *plentiful*.
A new pair of gloves.	A *pair of new* gloves.
A young beautiful woman.	A *beautiful young* woman.
Where do you come from?	*Whence* do you come?
Where are you going?	*Whither* are you going?
For such another fault.	*For another such* fault.
Of consequence.	Consequently.
Having not considered it.	Not having considered it.
I had rather not.	I *would* rather not.
I'd as lief.	I would *as soon*.
For good and all.	Totally and completely.
This here house, said I.	This house, *said* I.
Where is it? says I, to him.	Where is it? *said* I, to him.
I propose to visit them.	I *purpose* to visit them.
He spoke contemptibly of me.	He spoke *contemptuously* of me.
It is apparent.	It is *obvious*.
In its primary sense.	In its *primitive* sense.
I heard them *pro & con*.	I heard *both sides*.
I an't hungry.	I *am not* hungry.
I want a scissors.	I want a *pair of* scissors.
A new pair of shoes.	A *pair of new* shoes.
saw him some ten years ago.	I saw him ten years ago.
I met in with him.	I *met with* him.
The subject matter.	The subject.
I add one more reason.	I add *one reason more*.

IMPROPER EXPRESSIONS.

Do you find how many chapters are in Job?—*remember.*
His public character is undeniable—*unexceptionable.*
The wool is cheaper;—but the cloth is as dear as ever—*omit the* in both places.
They gained five shillings the piece by it—*a piece.*
It is not worth a sixpence—*sixpence.*
A letter conceived in the following words—*expressed.*
He is much difficulted—*at a loss, puzzled.*
He behaved in a very gentlemanny manner—*gentleman-like.*
The poor boy was ill-guided—*ill-used.*
There was a great many company—*much company.*
He has been misfortunate—*unfortunate.*
A momentuous circumstance—*momentous.*
You will some day repent it—*one day repent of it.*
Severals were of that opinion—*Several, i. e. several persons.*
He did it in an overly manner—*in a careless.*
He does every thing pointedly—*exactly.*
An honest like man—*A tall good-looking man.*
At the expiry of his lease—*expiration.*
If I had ever so much in my offer—*choice.*
Have you any word to your brother?—*message.*
The cock is a noisy beast—*fowl.*
Are you acquaint with him?—*acquainted.*
Were you crying on me?—*calling.*
Direct your letters to me at Mr. B.'s, Edinburgh—*Address.*
He and I never cast out—*never quarrel.*
He took a fever—*was seized with a fever.*
He was lost in the river—*drowned* (if the body was got.)
That militates against your doctrine—*operates.*
If I am not mistaken—*If I mistake not.*
You may lay your account with opposition—*You may expect.*
He proposes to buy an estate—*purposes.*
He plead his own cause—*pleaded.*
Have ye plenished your house?—*furnished.*
I shall notice a few particulars—*mention.*
I think much shame—*I am much ashamed.*
Will I help you to a bit of beef?—*Shall.*
They wared their money to advantage—*laid out.*
Will we see you next week?—*Shall.*
She thinks long to see him—*She longs to see him.*
It is not that much worth—*It is not worth much.*

IMPROPER EXPRESSIONS.

Is ging to the school?—*to school.* Go and pull berries—*gather.*
Be has got the cold—*a cold.* Pull roses—*Pluck* or *gather.*
Say the grace—*Say grace.* To harry a nest—*rob.*
I cannot go the day—*to-day.* He begins to make rich—*grow.*
A four square table—*A square table.* Mask the tea—*Infuse.*
He is cripple—*lame.* I was maltreated—*ill used.*
Get my big coat—*great coat.* He mants much—*stammers.*
Hard fish—*Dried fish.* I see'd him yesterday—*saw.*
A novel fashion—*new.* A house to lot—*to be let.*—K.p.86.3
He is too precipitant—*hasty.* Did you tell upon him—*inform.*
Roasted cheese—*Toasted.* Come here—*hither.*
I dinna ken—*I don't know.* A house to sell—*to be sold.*—K.p.84
Sweet butter—*Fresh.* I knowed that—*knew.*
I have a sore head—*head-ache.* That dress sets her—*becomes.*
A stupendous work—*stupendous.* She turned sick—*grew.*
A tremendous work—*tremendous.* He is turned tall—*grown.*
I got timous notice—*timely.* This here boy—*This boy.*
A summer's day—*summer day.* It is equally the same—*It is the same.*
An oldish lady—*elderly.* It is split new—*quite.*
A few broth—*Some.** That there man—*That man.*
I have nothing ado—*to do.* What pretty it is!—*How.*
Ass milk—*Ass's.* His is for mester—*mush.*
Take a drink—*draught.* That's no possible—*not.*
A pair of partridges—*A brace.* I shall go the morn—*to-morrow.*
Six horse—*horses.* I asked at him—*asked him.*
A milk cow—*milch.* Is your papa in?—*within.*
Send me a swatch—*pattern.* He was married on—*to.*
He lays in bed till nine—*lies.* Come in to the fire—*nearer.*
I mind none of them things—*those.* Take out your glass—*off.*
Give me them books—*these.* I find no fault to him—*in.*
Close the door—*Shut.* Cheese and bread—*Bread and cheese.*
Let him be—*alone.* Milk and bread—*Bread and milk.*
Call for James—*on.*—p. 112, b. † Take tent—*Take care.*
Chap louder—*Knock.* Come, say away—*Come, proceed.*
I find no pain—*feel.* Do bidding—*Be obedient.*
I mean to summons—*summon.* He is a widow—*widower.*
Will I help you?—*Shall.* He stops there—*stays, dwells, lodges.*
Shall James come again?—*Will.* Shall they return soon?—*Will.*
He has a timber leg—*a wooden.* Will we go home now?—*Shall.*
are angry—*I am not.* He misguides his book—*abuses.*
Tha... bare house—*That house.* He don't do it well—*does not.*

---

* Broth is always singular—Powdered beef is beef sprinkled with salt, to preserve it for a few days. Salt beef is beef properly seasoned with salt.

Miscellaneous Observations.

Additional Remarks under the 4th Rule of Syntax

1. When *and* is *understood*, the verb must be plural; as, Wisdom, happiness, (and) virtue, *dwell* with the golden mediocrity.

Some think, that when two singular nouns, coupled with *and*, are nearly the same in meaning, the verb may be singular; as, Tranquillity and peace *dwells* there. Ignorance and negligence *has* produced this effect. This, however, is improper; for *tranquillity* and *peace* are *two* nouns or names and two make a *plural*; therefore the verb should be plural.

2. Two or more singular nouns coupled with *and* require a verb in the *singular* number, when they denote only *one* person or thing; as, That able scholar and critic *has* been eminently useful.

3. Many writers use a *plural noun* after the 2nd of two numerical adjectives; thus, The first and second *pages* are torn. This I think improper: it should rather be, The first and second *page*, i. e. the first *page* and the second *page* are torn:—*are,* perhaps; because independently of *and*, they are *both* in a torn state.——*Generation, hour,* and *ward* are singular in Exodus xx, 5. Matt. xx, 5. Acts xii, 10.

And and *Not*.

4. When *not* is joined to *and*, the negative clause forms a parenthesis, and does not affect the construction of the other clause or clauses; therefore, the verb in the following and similar sentences should be singular. Genuine piety, and not great riches, *makes* a death-bed easy; i. e. Genuine piety

MISCELLANEOUS OBSERVATIONS.

makes a death-bed easy, and great riches do no*r* *make* it easy. Her prudence, not her possession*s* *renders* her an object of desire.

Every, And.

5. When the nouns coupled with *and* are qua lified by the distributive *every*, the verb should be *singular;* as, Every man and woman *was* aston ished at her fortitude. Every boy and girl *wa*. taught to read.—See Rule 27th.

With and *And*.

6. When a *singular* noun has a clause joined t' it by *with*, it is often difficult to determine whethe the *verb* should be *singular* or *plural*, especially a our most reputable authors use sometimes the on and sometimes the other: for example, some woul say, My uncle, with his son, *was* in town yester day. Others would say, My uncle, with his son *were* in town yesterday.

If we take the *sense* for our guide, and nothing else can guide us in a case of this kind, it is evi dent that the verb should be *plural;* for both *uncle* and *son* are the *joint* subjects of our affirmation and declared to be both in the *same* state.

When we perceive from the sense, that the noun *before With* is *exclusively* the real subject, then the verb should be *singular;* thus, *Christ*, with his three chosen disciples, *was* transfigured on the mount Here the verb is singular, because we know that none but Christ was transfigured; the disciples were not *joint* associates with him; they were mere spec tators. There seems to be an ellipsis in such sen tences as this, which, if supplied in the present

MISCELLANEOUS OBSERVATIONS.

would run thus: Christ, (who was attended) with his three chosen disciples, was transfigured on the mount.

Mr. Murray, however, thinks that the verb should be *singular* in the following and similar sentences. "Prosperity, with humility, *renders its* possessors truly amiable." "The side A, with the sides B and C, *composes* the triangle." In my opinion, on the contrary, the verb should be *plural*. For, in the first sentence, it is not asserted that prosperity *alone* renders its possessor truly amiable, but prosperity and humility *united*, and co-operating to produce an effect in their *joint* state, which they were incapable of achieving in their *individual* capacity.

If true, as Mr. Murray says, that "the *side A*," in the second sentence, is the *true* nominative to the verb, then it follows, of course, that the two sides, B and C, have no agency or no share in forming the triangle, and consequently that the side A *alone* composes the triangle. It is obvious, however, that *one* side cannot form a triangle or three-sided figure, and that the sides B and C are as much concerned in forming the triangle as the side A, and therefore the verb should be *plural*.

Upon the whole, we may venture to give the two following general rules.

1. That wherever the noun or pronoun *after With* exists, acts, or suffers *jointly* with the singular nominative *before* it, the verb should be *plural*; as, "She with her sisters *are* well." "His purse, with its contents, *were* abstracted from his pocket." "The general with his men *were* taken prisoners." In these sentences the verb is *plural*, because the words *after With* are as much the

MISCELLANEOUS OBSERVATIONS.

subject of discourse as the words *before* it,—her *sisters* were *well* as well as she; the *contents,* as well as the purse, were abstracted; and the *men,* as well as the general, were taken prisoners. If, in the first example, we say,—*is* well, then the meaning will be, she is well when in *company* with her sisters; and the idea that her *sisters* are *well,* will be entirely *excluded.*

2. When the noun after *with* is a mere involuntary or inanimate *instrument,* the verb should be *singular;* as, The Captain with his men *catches* poor Africans and *sells* them for slaves. The Squire with his hounds *kills* a fox. Here the verb is *singular,* because the men and hounds are no *joint* agents with the Captain and Squire; they are as much the mere instruments in their hands as the *gun* and *pen* in the hands of He and She in the following sentences. He with his gun *shoots* a hare. She with her pen *writes* a letter.

Of the Articles, with several Adjectives.

A or *the* is prefixed only to the first of several adjectives qualifying one noun: as, A meek and holy man: but the article should be repeated, before each adjective, when each adjective relates to a generic word applicable to every one of the adjectives. For example, "The black and white cows were sold yesterday; the red will be sold to-morrow."

Here cows is the *generic* word, applicable to each of the adjectives, *black, white,* and *red,* but for want of *the* before *white,* we are led to suppose that the *black* and *white* cows mean only *one* sort, which are speckled with spots of black and white; and if this is our meaning, the sentence

MISCELLANEOUS OBSERVATIONS.

s right; but if we mean *two* different sorts, the one all black and the other all white, we should insert the article before both; and say, *The* black and *the* white cows, *i. e.* The black cows and the white cows were sold.

Some think this distinction of little importance; and it is really seldom attended to even by good writers; but in some cases it is necessary; although in others there cannot, from the nature of the thing, be any mistake. In the following sentence, for instance, the repetition of *the* before *horned* is not *necessary,* although it would be proper. "The *bald* and *horned* cows were sold last week." Here there can be no mistake, *two* sorts were sold; for a cow cannot be bald and horned too.

The same remark may be made respecting the *Demonstrative* pronouns that has been made respecting the *articles;* as, "*That* great and good man," means only *one* man: but *that* great and *that* good man would mean *two* men; the one a *great* man, the other a *good.*

They—Those.

They stands for a noun already introduced, and should never be used till the noun be mentioned. *Those,* on the contrary, points out a noun not previously introduced, but generally understood. It is improper therefore to say, *They* who tell lies are never esteemed. *They* that are truly good must be happy. We should say, *Those* who tell lies, and *those* that are truly good; because we are *pointing out* a particular class of persons, and not *referring* to nouns previously introduced. A noun

K

MISCELLANEOUS OBSERVATIONS.

when not expressed after *this, that, these,* and *thos* is always understood.

Another—One—Every.

Another corresponds to *one;* but not to *some* nor to *every.* Thus, "Handed down from *every* writer of verses to *another,*" should be, from *one* writer of verses to *another.* "At *some* hour or *another,*" should be, At *some* hour or *other.*

One is often used in familiar phrases (like *on* in French) for *we* or any *one* of us indiscriminately: thus, *One* is often more influenced by example than by precept. The verb and pronoun with which *one* agrees should be *singular.* Thus, If *one* take a wrong method at first, it will lead *them* astray: should be, it will lead *one* astray, or, it will lead *him* astray.

That and *Those*

It is improper to apply *that* and *those* to things *present* or just *mentioned.* Thus, "They cannot be separated from the subject which follows; and for *that* reason," &c.; should be, and for *this* reason, &c. "*Those* sentences which we have at present before us;" should be, *These,* or, *The* sentences which we have, &c.

As follows, as appears.

As is often used as a Personal or Relative pronoun, and in both *numbers,* and in these cases it should be construed as a pronoun: as, "His words were as *follow,*" that is, His words were *those* which follow. Here *as* is *plural,* because *words,* its antecedent, is plural. His description was as *follows.* Here *as* is *singular,* because *description,* its antecedent, is singular; that is, His description was *this which* follows.

MISCELLANEOUS OBSERVATIONS.

This account of *as*, though in unison with Dr Crombie's, is at variance with that of Dr. Campbell and Mr. Murray. They explain the following sentences thus: "The arguments advanced were nearly *as follows;*" "The positions were *as appears* incontrovertible." That is, say they, "as *it follows,*" "as *it appears.*" What *it?* The *thing*. What thing?—*It*, or thing, cannot relate to *arguments*, for arguments is *plural*, and must have a plural pronoun and verb. Take the ordinary method of finding out the nominative to a verb, by asking a question with the verb, and the true nominative will be the answer: Thus, What follows? and the answer is, The *arguments follow*. It must be obvious, then, that *it* cannot be substituted for *arguments*, and that *as* is equal to *those which*, and that the verb is not, *impersonal*, but the *third person* plural, agreeing with its nominative *which*, the last half of *as*. In the second example, *as appears* is a mere parenthesis, and does not relate to *positions* at all, but still the *as* is a pronoun. Thus, The positions, *it appears*, were incontrovertible.

They say, however, if we use *such* before *as*, the verb is no longer *impersonal*, but agrees with its nominative in the *plural* number; as, "The arguments advanced were nearly *such as follow.*" "The positions were such as *appear* incontrovertible." This is, if possible, a greater mistake than the former; for what has *such* to do with the following verb? *Such* means *of that kind*, and expresses the quality of the *noun* repeated, but it has nothing to do with the verb at all. Therefore the construction must be the same with *such* that it is with *as*

MISCELLANEOUS OBSERVATIONS.

this difference in meaning, that when *such as* is used, we mean of *that kind* which follows.

When we say, " His arguments are as *follow*,' we mean *those* arguments which follow are *verbatim* the very *same* that he used; but when we say, " His arguments were *such* as follow," we convey the idea, that the arguments which follow are *not* the very *same* that he used; but that they are only of the same *nature* or *kind*.

Their position, however, that the verb should be plural, can be made out by a circumlocution, thus: " His arguments were nearly *such* arguments as those which follow are:" but this very solution would show the error into which they have fallen in such phrases as, *as follows, as appears,* for they will not admit of similar solutions. We cannot say, " His arguments are nearly as the arguments which *follows is.*"*

This means, &c

The word *means* in the singular number, and the phrases, *By this means, By that means,* are used by our best and most correct writers, when they denote instrumentality; as, By *means of death,* &c. By *that means* he preserves his superiority —*Addison*.

Good writers use the noun *mean* in the singular number, only to denote *mediocrity, middle state,* &c. as, This is a *mean* between the two extremes.

This means and *that means*, should be used only when they refer to what is singular; *these means,*

---

* Addison and Steele have used a *plural verb* where the antecedent to *as* is plural. See Tattler, No. 62, 104.—Spect. No. 513. Dr. Campbell, in his Philosophy of Rhetoric, vol. ii, p. 7, has mistaken the construction of these phrases.

MISCELLANEOUS OBSERVATIONS.

when they refer to what is singular; *these means* and *those means*, when they respect plurals; as, He lived temperately, and by this means preserved his health. The scholars were attentive, industrious, and obedient to their tutors; and by *these means* acquired knowledge.

Amends.

Amends is used in the same manner as *means*; as, Peace of mind is *an* honourable *amends* for the sacrifices of interest. In return, he received the thanks of his employers, and the present of a large estate: *these* were ample *amends* for all his labours

Into, in.

Into is used after a verb of motion: and *in*, when motion or rest *in* a place is signified; as, They *cast* him *into* a pit; I walk *in* the park.

So and such.

When we refer to the *species* or *nature* of a thing, the word *such* is properly applied; as, *Such* a temper is seldom found; but when *degree* is signified, we use the word *so*; as, *So* bad a temper is seldom found.

Disappointed of, disappointed in.

We are disappointed *of* a thing, when we do not get it, and disappointed *in* it when we have it, and find that it does not answer our expectations; as, We are often disappointed *in* things, which, before possession, promised much enjoyment. I have frequently desired their company, but have hitherto been disappointed *of* that pleasure.

MISCELLANEOUS OBSERVATIONS.

Taste of, and *taste* for.

A taste *of* a thing, implies actual enjoyment of it; but a taste *for* it, implies only a capacity for enjoyment; as, When we have had a true taste *of* the pleasures of virtue, we can have no relish *for* those of vice. He had a taste *for* such studies, and pursued them earnestly.

The Nominative and the Verb.

When the nominative case has no personal tense of a verb, but is put before a participle, independent of the rest of the sentence, it is called the *case absolute*; as, *Shame* being lost, all virtue is lost; *him* destroyed; *him* descending: *him* only excepted;—*him*, in all these places, should be *he*.

Every *verb*, except in the infinitive mood or the participle, ought to have a *nominative* case, either expressed or implied; as, *Arise*, let us go hence; that is, *Arise ye.*

Every *nominative* case should belong to some *verb*, either expressed or implied, as; To whom thus *Adam*, i. e. *spoke*. In the following sentence, the word *virtue* is left by itself, without any verb with which it might agree. " Virtue, however it may be neglected for a time, men are so constituted, as ultimately to acknowledge and respect genuine merit:" it should be, However *much virtue may* be neglected, &c. The sentence may be made more elegant by altering the arrangement of the words: thus, Such is the constitution of men, *that virtue*, however much it may be neglected for a time, *will* ultimately be acknowledged and respected.—*See Rule* XIX

The nominative is commonly placed *before* the

MISCELLANEOUS OBSERVATIONS.

verb ; but it is sometimes put *after* it, or between the auxiliary and the verb.—See Parsing, No. *e.*

Them is sometimes improperly used instead of *these* or *those* ; as, Give me *them* books, for *those* books, or *these* books.

What is sometimes improperly used for *that* ; as, They will never believe but *what* I have been to blame ; it should be—but *that* I have been, &c.

Which is often improperly used for *that* ; thus After *which* time, should be, After *that* time.

Which is applied to *collective* nouns composed of men ; as, The *court* of Spain *which* ; the company *which,* &c.

Which, and not *who,* should be used after the name of a person used merely as a *word* ; as, The court of Queen Elizabeth, *who* was but another name for prudence and economy ; it should be, *which* was but another, or, *whose name* was, &c.

It is and *it was* are often used in plural construction, as, *It is* they that are the real authors *It was* the heretics that first began to rail, &c.—*They are* the real authors. The *heretics* first began, &c., would perhaps be more elegant.

The neuter pronoun *it* is frequently joined to a noun or pronoun of the masculine or feminine gender ; as, *It* was *I* ; *It* was the *man.*

Adjectives, in many cases, should not be separated from their nouns, even by words which modify their meaning ; thus, A large enough number ; A distinct enough manner ; should be, A number large enough ; A manner distinct enough. The *adjective* is frequently placed *after* the noun which it qualifies ; as, Goodness *divine* ; Alexander the *Great.*

MISCELLANEOUS OBSERVATIONS.

All is sometimes emphatically put after a number of particulars comprehended under it; as, Ambition, interest, honour, *all* these concurred.

Never generally precedes the verb; as, I *never* saw him: but when an auxiliary is used, *never* may be placed either between it and the verb, or before both; as, He was *never* seen, or, He never was seen.

The *present participle* is frequently introduced without any obvious reference to any *noun* or *pronoun*; as, Generally *speaking*, he behaves well. *Granting* his story to be true, &c. A pronoun is perhaps understood; as, *We* speaking; *We* granting.

Sometimes a *neuter* verb governs an objective, when the noun is of the same import with the verb; thus, to dream a *dream;* to run a *race.* Sometimes the noun after a neuter verb is governed by a preposition understood; as, He lay six hours in bed, i. e. *during* six hours.

The same verbs are sometimes used as *active,* and sometimes as *neuter,* according to the sense; thus, *Think,* in the phrase, "*Think* on me," is a *neuter* verb; but it is active in the phrase, "Charity *thinketh* no evil."

It is improper to change the form of the second and third person singular of the auxiliaries in the *compound tenses* of the subjunctive mood; thus, If thou *have* done thy duty. Unless he *have* brought money. If thou *had* studied more diligently. Unless thou *shall* go to-day. If thou *will* grant my request, &c., should be, If thou *hast* done thy duty Unless he *has* brought. If thou *hadst* studied Unless thou *shalt* go, &c.

MISCELLANEOUS OBSERVATIONS.

It is improper to vary the second person singular in the *past* subjunctive, (except the verb *to be*;) thus, If thou *came* not in time, &c. If thou *did* not submit, &c., *should be*. If thou *camest* not in time; If thou *didst* not submit.

The following phrases, selected from the Scriptures, are strictly grammatical.

If thou *knewest* the gift. *If* thou *didst* receive it. *If* thou *hadst* known. *If* thou *wilt* save Israel. *Though* he *hath* escaped the sea. *That* thou *mayst* be feared. We also properly say, *If* thou *mayst mightst, couldst, wouldst,* or *shouldst* love.

OF CAPITALS.

1. The first word of every book, or any other piece of writing, must begin with a capital letter.
2. The first word after a period, and the answer to a question, must begin, &c.
3. Proper names, that is, names of persons, places, ships, &c.
4. The pronoun *I*, and the interjection *O*, are written in capitals.
5. The first word of every line in poetry.
6. The appellations of the Deity, as, God, Most High, &c.
7. Adjectives derived from the proper names of places; as, Grecian, Roman, English, &c.
8. The first word of a quotation, introduced after a colon; as, Always remember this ancient maxim; "*Know* thyself."
9. Common nouns when personified; as, Como, gentle *Spring*.

Directions for Superscriptions, and Forms of Address to Persons of every Rank.

To the King's Most Excellent Majesty,—*Sire*, or *May it please your Majesty.*—Conclude a petition or speech with, Your Majesty's most Loyal and Dutiful Subject.

To the Queen's Most Excellent Majesty,—*Madam*, or *May it please your Majesty.*

To his Royal Highness, Frederick, Duke of York,—*May it please your Royal Highness.*

To his Royal Highness the Duke of Kent,—*May it please your Royal Highness.*

In the same manner address every other of the Royal Family, *male or female.*

NOBILITY.—To his Grace the Duke of ——, †—*My Lord Duke, Your Grace,* or *May it please your Grace.*

To the Most Noble the Marquis of ——,—*My Lord Marquis, Your Lordship.*

To the Right Honourable —— Earl of ——,—*My Lord, Your Lordship.*

To the Right Honourable Lord Viscount ——,—*My Lord, Your Lordship.*

To the Right Honourable Baron ——,—*My Lord, May it please your Lordship.*

The wives of Noblemen have the same titles with their husbands, thus:

To her Grace the Dutchess of ——,—*May it please your Grace.*

To the Right Honourable Lady Ann Rose,—*My Lady, May it please your Ladyship.*

The titles of *Lord* and *Right Honourable* are given to all the sons of *Dukes* and *Marquises,* and to the eldest sons of *Earls;* and the title of *Lady* and *Right Honourable* to all their daughters. The *younger* sons of *Earls* are all *Honourable* and *Esquires.*

---

* The *superscription*, or what is put on the *outside* of letter, is printed in Roman characters, and begins with *To.* The terms of *address* used either in *beginning* a letter, a petition, or verbal address are printed in *Italic* letters immediately after the superscription.

† The *blanks* are to be filled up with the *real* name and title.

Forms of Address.

Right Honourable is due to Earls, Viscounts, and Barons, and to all the members of his Majesty's Most* Honourable Privy Council—To the Lord Mayor of *London*, *York*, and *Dublin* and to the Lord Provost of *Edinburgh*, during the time they are in *office*—To the Speaker of the House of Commons—To the Lords Commissioners of the Treasury, Admiralty, Trade, and Plantations, &c.

The House of Peers is addressed thus, To the Right Honourable the Lords Spiritual and Temporal of the United Kingdom of Great Britain and Ireland in Parliament assembled,—*My Lords, May it please your Lordships.*

The House of Commons is addressed thus, To the Honourable the Knights, Citizens, and Burgesses of the United Kingdom of Great Britain and Ireland in Parliament assembled,—*Gentlemen, May it please your Honours.*

The sons of Viscounts and Barons are styled Honourable and Esquires; and their daughters have their letters addressed thus, To the Honourable Miss or Mrs. D. B.

The king's commission confers the title of Honourable on any gentleman in a place of honour or trust; such as the Commissioners of Excise, His Majesty's Customs, Board of Control, &c.—Admirals of the Navy—Generals, Lieutenant-Generals, and Colonels in the Army.

All Noblemen, or men of title in the Army or Navy, use their title by *right*, such as *honourable*, before their title of *rank* such as *captain*, &c., thus, the *Honourable Captain* James James of the ——— *Sir, Your Honour.*

Honourable is due also to the Court of Directors of the East India Company—the Governors and Deputy Governors of the Bank of England.

The title *Excellency* is given to all Ambassadors, Plenipotentiaries, Governors in foreign countries, to the Lord Lieutenant, and to the Lords Justices of the Kingdom of Ireland.— Address such thus :

To his Excellency Sir ——— Bart. his Britannic Majesty's Envoy Extraordinary, and Plenipotentiary to the Court of Reice, —*Your Excellency, May it please your Excellency.*

---

* The Privy Counsellors, taken collectively, are styled his Majesty's Most Honourable Privy Council

FORMS OF ADDRESS.

The title, *Right Worshipful*, is given to the Sheriffs, Aldermen and Recorder of London; and *Worshipful* to the Aldermen and Recorders of other Corporations, and to Justices of the Peace in England,—*Sir, Your Worship.*

The Clergy are all styled *Reverend*, except the Archbishops and Bishops, who have something additional; thus,—

To his Grace the Archbishop of Canterbury; or, To the *Most Reverend Father in God, Charles, Lord Archbishop of Canterbury,—My Lord, Your Grace.*

To the *Right* Reverend Father in God, John, Lord Bishop of ———, *My Lord, Your Lordship.*

To the Very Rev. Dr. A. B., Dean of ———, *Sir.* To the Rev. Mr. Desk; or, To the Rev. John Desk.*

The general address to Clergymen is, *Sir,* and when written to, *Reverend Sir.*—Deans and Archdeacons are usually styled *Very Reverend,* and called *Mr. Dean, Mr. Archdeacon.*

Address the Principal of the University of Edinburgh, thus; To the Very Rev. Dr. B., Principal of the University of Edinburgh.—*Doctor;* when written to, *Very Rev. Doctor.* The other Professors thus; To Dr. D. R., Professor of Logic in the University of E.—*Doctor.* If a Clergyman, say, To the Rev. Dr. J. M., Professor of, &c.—*Reverend Doctor.*

Those who are not *Drs* are styled *Esquire*, but not Mr. too: thus, To J. P., Esq., Professor of Humanity in the University of Edinburgh,—*Sir.* If he has a literary title, it may be added, thus, To J. P., Esq., A. M., Professor of, &c.

Magistrates, Barristers at Law or Advocates, and Members of Parliament, viz. of the House of Commons, (these last have *M. P.* after *Esq.,*) and all gentlemen in independent circumstances, are styled *Esquire,* and their wives *Mrs.*

---

* It seems to be unsettled whether *Mr.* should be used after *Reverend* or not. In my opinion it should; because it gives a clergyman his own honorary title over and above the common one. May we not use the Rev. Mr. as well as the Rev. Dr.? Besides, we do not always recollect whether his name is *James* or *John*, &c. Mr., in such a case, would look better on the back of a letter than a long ill-drawn dash, thus, The Rev. ——— Desk. In short, *Mr.* is used by our best writers after Reverend, but not uniformly. The words *To the*, not being necessary on the *back* of a letter, are seldom used; but in addressing it in the *inside*, left hand corner, at the bottom, they are generally used. In addressing *bills* they are necessary

Punctuation.

Punctuation is the art of pointing written composition in such a manner as may naturally lead to its proper meaning, construction, and delivery.

Of the Comma.

Rule I.

A simple sentence in general requires only a full stop at the end; as, True politeness has its seat in the heart.

Rule II.

The simple members of a compound sentence are separated by a comma; as, Crafty men contemn studies, simple men admire them, and wise men use them. He studies diligently, and makes great progress.

Rule III.

The persons in a direct address are separated from the rest of the sentence by commas; as, *My son,* give me thine heart. *Colonel,* Your most obedient. I thank you, *sir.* I am obliged to you, *my friends,* for your kindness.

Rule IV.

Two words of the same part of speech, whether nouns, adjectives, verbs, participles, or adverbs do not admit of a comma between them, when coupled with a conjunction; as, James *and* John are good. She is wise *and* virtuous. Religion expands *and* elevates the mind. By being admired *and* flattered, she became vain. Cicero spoke forcibly *and* fluently. When the conjunction is suppressed, a comma is inserted in its place; as, He was a plain, honest man.

Of the Comma.

RULE V.

Three or more nouns, adjectives, verbs, participles, or adverbs, are separated by commas: as, The sun, the moon, and the stars, are the glory of nature.

When words follow in *pairs*, there is a comma between each *pair*; as, Truth is fair and artless, simple and sincere, uniform and constant.

RULE VI.

All phrases or explanatory sentences, whether in the beginning, middle, or end of a simple sentence, are separated from it by commas; as, To confess the truth, I was in fault. His father dying, he succeeded to the estate. The king, approving the plan, put it into execution. Paul, the apostle of the Gentiles, was eminent for his zeal and knowledge. George the Third, king of Great Britain. I have seen the emperor, as he was called. In short, he was a great man.

RULE VII.

The verb *to be*, followed by an adjective, or an infinitive with adjuncts, is generally preceded by a comma; as, To be diligently employed in the performance of real duty, is honourable. One of the noblest of the Christian virtues, is to love our enemies.*

RULE VIII.

A comma is used between the two parts of a sentence that has its natural order inverted; as, Him that is weak in the faith, receive ye.

---

* Some insert a comma both *before* and *after* the verb *to be* when is near the middle of a long sentence, because the *pronunciation* requires it, but that is a bad reason; for pauses and points are often at variance.

Of the Comma.

Rule IX.

Any remarkable expression resembling a quotation or a command, is preceded by a comma as. There is much truth in the proverb *Without* pains no gains. I say unto all, *Watch*.

Rule X.

Relative pronouns admit of a comma before them in some cases, and in some not.

When several words come between the relative and its antecedent,* a comma is inserted; but not in other cases: as, There is no *charm* in the female sex, *which can supply* the place of virtue. It is labour only *which gives* the relish to pleasure. The first *beauty* of style is propriety, *without which* all ornament is puerile and superfluous. It is barbarous to injure those *from whom* we have received a kindness.

Rule XI.

A comma is often inserted where a verb is *understood*, and particularly before *not*, *but*, and *though*, in such cases as the following; as, John has acquired much knowledge; his brother, (has acquired) little. A man ought to obey reason *not* appetite. He was a great poet, *but* a bad man. The sun is up, *though* he is not visible.

A comma is sometimes inserted between the two members of a *long* sentence connected by comparatives; as, Better is little with the fear of the Lord, than great treasure and trouble therewith. As thy days, so shall thy strength be.

---

* That is, when the relative clause is merely *explanatory*, the relative is preceded by a comma.

Of the Comma.
Rule XII.

It has been stated, in Rule VI., that explanatory words and phrases, such as *perfectly, indeed doubtless, formerly, in fine,* &c., should be separated from the context by a comma.

Many adverbs, however, and even phrases, when they are considered of little importance, should *not* be separated from the rest of the sentence by commas; as, Be ye *therefore* perfect. *Peradventure* ten shall be found there. All things *indeed* are pure. *Doubtless* thou art our father. They were *formerly* very studious. He was *at last* convinced of his error. Be not ye *therefore* partakers with them. *Nevertheless* the poor man's wisdom is despised. Anger is *in a manner* like madness. *At length* some pity warmed the master's breast.

These twelve rules respecting the position of the *comma*, include every thing, it is presumed, to be found in the more numerous rules of larger volumes. But it is impossible to make them perfect. For, "In many instances the employment or omission of a comma, depends upon the length or the shortness of a clause; the presence or absence of adjuncts; the importance or non-importance of the sentiment. Indeed, with respect to punctuation, the practice of the best writers is extremely arbitrary; many omitting some of the usual commas when no error in sense, or in construction, is likely to arise from the omission. Good sense and attentive observation are more likely to regulate this subject than any mechanical directions.

The best general rule is, to point in such a manner as to make the sense evident.

☞ No exercises have been subjoined to the Rules on punctuation because none can be given equal to those the pupil can prescribe for himself. After he has learned the Rules, let him transcribe a piece from any good author, omitting the points and capitals, and then, having pointed his manuscript, and restored the capitals, let him compare his own punctuation with the author's.

Of the Semicolon.

The semicolon is used to separate two members of a sentence less dependent on each other than those separated by the comma.

Sometimes the two members have a mutual dependence on one another, both in sense and syntax, sometimes the preceding member makes complete sense of itself, and only the following one is dependent; and sometimes both seem to be independent.

EXAMPLES

As coals are to burning coals, and wood to fire; so is a contentious man to kindle strife. As a roaring lion and a ranging bear; so is a wicked ruler over the poor people. Mercy and truth preserve the king; and his throne is upheld by mercy. He that loveth pleasure shall be a poor man; he that loveth wine and oil shall not be rich. Philosophy asserts, that Nature is unlimited in her operations; that she has inexhaustible stores in reserve; that knowledge will always be progressive; and that all future generations will continue to make discoveries, of which we have not the least idea.

The semicolon is sometimes employed to separate simple members in which even no commas occur: thus, The pride of wealth is contemptible; the pride of learning is pitiable; the pride of dignity is ridiculous; and the pride of bigotry is insupportable.

In every one of these members the construction and sense are complete; and a period might have been used instead of the semicolon; which is preferred merely because the sentences are short and form a climax.

L

Of the Colon.

The colon is used when the preceding part of the sentence is complete in sense and construction; and the following part is some remark naturally arising from it, and depending on it in sense, though not in construction; as, Study to acquire the habit of thinking: no study is more important.

A colon is generally used before an example or a quotation; as, The Scriptures give us an amiable representation of the Deity in these words: God is love. He was often heard to say: I have done with the world, and I am willing to leave it.

A colon is generally used where the sense is complete in the first clause, and the next begins with a conjunction *understood*; as, Do not flatter yourselves with the hope of perfect happiness there is no such thing in the world. Had the conjunction *for* been expressed, a semicolon would have been used; thus, Do not flatter yourselves with the hope of perfect happiness; *for* there is no such thing in the world.

The *colon* is generally used when the conjunction is *understood*; and the *semicolon*, when the conjunction is *expressed*.

NOTE. This observation has not always been attended to in pointing the Psalms and some parts of the Liturgy. In them, a colon is often used merely to divide the verse, it would seem, into two parts, to suit a particular species of church-music called *chanting*; as, "My tongue is the pen: of a ready writer." In reading, a cesural pause, in such a place as this, is enough. In the Psalms, and often in the Proverbs, the colon must be read like a semicolon, or even like a comma according to the sense.

Of the Period.

When a sentence is complete in construction and sense, it is marked with a period; as, Jesus wept.

A period is sometimes admitted between sentences connected by such words as *but, and, for, therefore, hence*, &c. Example: And he arose and came to his father. *But* when he was yet a great way off, &c.

All abbreviations end with a *period;* as, A. D

Of other Characters used in Composition.

Interrogation (?) is used when a question is asked.

Admiration (!) or *Exclamation*, is used to express any sudden emotion of the mind.

Parenthesis ( ) is used to enclose some necessary remark in the body of another sentence: commas are now used instead of Parentheses.

Apostrophe (') is used in place of a letter left out; as, *lov'd* for loved

Caret (ʌ) is used to show that some word is either omitted or interlined.

Hyphen (-) is used at the *end* of a *line*, to show that the rest of the word is at the beginning of the next line. It also connects compound words; as, *Tea-pot*.

Section (§) is used to divide a discourse or chapter into portions.

Paragraph (¶) is used to denote the beginning of a new subject.

Crotchets [ ], or *Brackets*, are used to enclose a word or sentence which is to be explained in a note, or the explanation itself, or to correct a mistake, or supply some deficiency.

Quotation (" ") is used to show that a passage is quoted in the author's words.

Index (☞) is used to point out any thing remarkable.

Brace { is used to connect words which have one common term, or three lines in poetry, having the *same* rhyme, called a triplet

Ellipsis (———) is used when some letters are omitted; as, K-g for King.

Acute accent (´) is used to denote a *short* syllable; the *grave* (`) a *long*

Breve (˘) marks a *short* vowel or syllable, and the dash (-) a *long*.

Diæresis (¨) is used to divide a diphthong into two syllables; as, aerial.

Asterisk (*) — *Obelisk* (†) — *Double dagger* (‡) — and *Parallels* (‖) with small letters and figures, refer to some note on the margin, or at the bottom of the page.

(***) Two or three asterisks denote the omission of some letters in some bold or indelicate expression.

Dash (———) is used to denote abruptness—a significant pause—an unexpected turn in the sentiment—or that the *first clause* is common to all the rest, as in this definition of a dash.

ABBREVIATIONS.

Latin.		English.
Ante Christum*	A.C.	Before Christ
Artium Baccalaureus	A.B.	Bachelor of Arts (often B. A.)
Anno Domini	A.D.	In the year of our Lord
Artium Magister	A.M.	Master of Arts
Anno Mundi	A.M	In the year of the world
Ante Meridiem	A.M.	In the forenoon
Anno Urbis Conditæ	A.U.C.	In the year after the building of the
Baccalaureus Divinitatis	B.D	Bachelor of Divinity [city—Rome
Custos Privati Sigilli	C.P.␣.	Keeper of the Privy Seal
Custos Sigilli	C.S.	Keeper of the Seal
Doctor Divinitatis	D.D	Doctor of Divinity
Exempli gratia	e.g.	For example
Regiæ Societatis Socius	R.S.˚	Fellow of the Royal Society
Regiæ Societatis Antiqua- riorum Socius	R.S.A	S. Fellow of the Royal Society of Antiquaries
Georgius Rex	G.R.	George the King
Id est	i.e.	That is
Jesus Hominum Salvator	J.H.S.	Jesus the Saviour of Men
Legum Doctor	LL.D.	Doctor of Laws
Messieurs (*French*,)	Messrs.	Gentlemen
Medicinæ Doctor	M.D.	Doctor of Medicine
Memoriæ Sacrum	M.S.	Sacred to the Memory (or S.M.)
Nota Bene	N.B.	Note well; Take notice
Post Meridiem	P.M.	In the afternoon
Post Scriptum	P.S.	Postscript, something written after
Ultimo	Ult.	Last (month)
Et Cætera	&c.	And the rest; and so forth

A.	Answer, Alexander	L.C.J.	Lord Chief Justice
Acct.	Account	Knt.	Knight
Bart.	Baronet	K.G.	Knight of the Garter
Bp.	Bishop	K.B.	Knight of the Bath
Capt.	Captain	K.C.B.	Knt. Commander of the Bath
Col.	Colonel	K.C.	Knt. of the Crescent
Cr.	Creditor	K.P.	Knight of St. Patrick
Dr.	Debtor, Doctor	K.T	Knight of the Thistle
Do. or Ditto.	The same.	MS.	Manuscript
Viz.†	Namely	MSS.	Manuscripts
Q.	Question, Queen	N.S.	New Style
R.N.	Royal Navy	O.S.	Old Style
Esq.	Esquire	J.P.	Justice of the Peace.

※ * The *Latin* of these abbreviations is inserted, not to be got by heart but to show the etymology of the English, and explain, for instance, how P.M. comes to mean afternoon, &c. — † Contracted for videlicet

PROSODY.

Prosody is that part of Grammar which teaches the true pronunciation of words; comprising Accent, Quantity, Emphasis, Pause and Tone, and the measure of Verses.

Accent is the laying of a greater force on one syllable of a word than on another; as, Surmount'.

The *quantity* of a syllable is that time which is occupied in pronouncing it. Quantity is either long or short; as, Cōnsūme.

Emphasis is a remarkable stress laid upon certain words in a sentence, to distinguish them from the rest, by making the meaning more apparent; as, Apply yourself more to *acquire* knowledge than to *show* it.*

A *pause* is either a total cessation or a short suspension of the voice, during a perceptible space of time; as, Reading-makes a full man; conference—a ready-man; and writing—an exact-man.

Tone is a particular modulation or inflection of the voice, suited to the sense; as, How bright these glorious spirits shine'†

Versification.

Prose is language not restrained to harmonic sounds, or to a set number of syllables.

Verse or *Poetry* is language restrained to a certain number of long and short syllables in every line.

Verse is of *two kinds;* namely, *Rhyme* and *Blank* verse. When the last syllable of every two lines has the same sound,

---

* *Emphasis* should be made rather by *suspending* the voice a little after the emphatic word, than by striking it very forcibly, which is disagreeable to a good ear. A very short pause before it would render it still more emphatical; as, Reading makes a—*full—*man.

† *Accent* and *quantity* respect the pronunciation of words, *emphasis* and *pause* the meaning of the sentence; while *tone* refers to the feelings of the speaker.

it is called *rhyme;* but when this is not the case, it is called *blank verse.*

Feet* are the parts into which a verse is divided, to see whether it has its just number of syllables or not.

Scanning is the measuring or dividing of a verse† into the several feet of which it is composed.

All feet consist either of *two* or *three* syllables, and are reducible to eight kinds; four of two syllables, and four of three, as follow :—

Dissyllables.	*Trissyllables.*
A trŏchēe; as, lŏvely.‡	A dactyle; as, prŏbăbly.
An ĭambus; bĕcāme.	An amphibrach; dŏmĕstĭc.
A spondee; vāin mān.	An anapaĕst; mĭsĭmprŏve.
A pyrrhic; ŏn ă (bank.)	A tribrach: (com)fŏrtăbly.

The feet in most common use are, Iambic, Trochaic, and Anapæstic.

Iambic Measure.

Iambic measure is adapted to serious subjects, and comprises verses of several kinds; such as,

1. *Of four syllables, or two feet; as,*

   Wĭth răv-ĭsh'd ĕars,
   Thĕ Mŏn-ărch hĕars.

It sometimes has an additional short syllable, making what is called a double ending; as,

   Upŏn-ă moun-tăin,
   Bĕsīde-ă fōun-tăin.

---

* So called from the resemblance which the movement of the tongue in reading verse, bears to the motion of the feet in walking.

† A single line is called a verse. In *rhyme* two lines are called a *couplet*; and three ending with the same sound a *triplet.*

‡ The marks over the vowels show that a *Trochee* consists of a *long* and a *short* syllable, and the Iambic of a *short* and a *long*, &c.

☞ In scanning verses, every *accented* syllable is called a *long* syllable; even although the sound of the vowel in pronunciation be *short.* Thus the first syllable in *rav-ish'd* is in scanning called a *long* syllable, although the vowel *a* is *short.* By *long* then is meant an *accented* syllable: and by *short*, an *unaccented* syllable.

2. *Of three iambics, or six syllables: as,*

> Aloft - in aw-ful state,
> The god-like hero sat,
> Our hearts-no long-er lan —guish.   An additional syllable.

3. *Of eight syllables, or four iambic feet; as,*

> And may - at last - my wea-ry age,
> Find out - the peace-ful her-mitage.

4. *Of ten syllables, or five feet; called hexameter, heroic, or tragic verses; as,*

> The stars - shall fade - away-the sun-himself
> Grow dim - with age, - and na-ture sink - in years.

Sometimes the last line of a couplet is stretched out to twelve syllables, or six feet, and then it is called an Alexandrine verse; as,

> For thee - the land - in fra-grant flow'rs - is drest;
> For thee - the o-cean smiles, - and smoothes - her wavy breast.

5. *Of verses containing alternately four and three feet, this is the measure commonly used in psalms and hymns; as,*

> Let saints - below, - with sweet - accord,
> Unite - with those - above,
> In so - lemn lays, to praise - their king
> And sing - his dy-ing love.

☞ Verses of this kind were anciently written in two lines, each containing fourteen syllables.

Trochaic Measure.

This measure is quick and lively, and comprises verses,

Some of one trochee and a long syllable, and some of two trochees; as,

> Tumult - cease,   On the - mountains
> Sink to - peace.   By a - fountain.

2. *Of two feet or two trochees with an additional long syllable; as*

    In thĕ - dāys ŏf - - ōld,
    Stŏrĭĕs - plāinly - - tōld.

3. *Of three trochees, or three and an additional long syllable. as*

    Whĕn ŏur - hĕārts ăre - mŏurnĭng,
    Lŏvely - lāstĭng - pĕace ŏf - - mĭnd,
    Swĕĕt dĕ - līght ŏf - hŭmăn - - kīnd.

4. *Of four trochees, or eight syllables; as,*

    Nŏw thĕ - drĕadfŭl - thŭndĕr's - rōarĭng!

5. *Of six trochees, or twelve syllables; as,*

    On ă mŏuntaĭn,-strĕtch'd bĕ - nĕath ă-hōary - wīllŏw
    Lăy ă - shĕphĕrd-swaĭn, ănd-vĭĕw'd thĕ - rōarĭng-bīllŏw.

Those trochaic measures that are very uncommon have been omitted.

Anapaestic Measure.

1. *Of two anapaests, or two and an unaccented syllable; as*

    Bŭt hĭs coŭr-ăge 'găn fāil,
    Fŏr nŏ ărts - coŭld ăvāil.
Or, Thĕn hĭs cour-age 'gan fail - - hĭm,
    For no arts - could avail - - hĭm.

2. *Of three anapaests, or nine syllables; as,*

    O yĕ wŏŏds - sprĕad yŏur brănch-ĕs ăpăce
    Tŏ yŏur dĕĕp-ĕst rĕcĕss-ĕs I fly;
    I wŏuld hĭde - wĭth thĕ bĕasts - ŏf thĕ chăse
    I wŏuld văn-ĭsh frŏm ĕv-ĕry eye

Sometimes a syllable is retrenched from the first foo, as

    Yĕ shĕp-hĕrds sŏ chĕĕr-fŭl ănd găy,
    Whŏse flŏcks   ĕvĕr căre-lĕssly rŏam.

3. *Of four anapaests, or twelve syllables.*

'Tis thē vōice - ŏf thē slŭg-gārd ; I hēar - hĭm cŏmplāin.
Yŏu hăve wāk'd - mē tŏŏ sōŏn, - I mŭst slŭm-bĕr ăgāin.

Sometimes an additional short syllable is found at the end ; as,

On thē wārm - chēek ŏf yŏuth, - smīles ănd rōs-ĕs, ăre blĕnd-ĭng.

The preceding are the different kinds of the Principal* feet in their more simple forms ; but they are susceptible of numerous variations, by mixing them with one another, and with the Secondary feet ; the following lines may serve as an example :—Spon. Amph., &c., *apply only to the first line.*

  Spon. Amph. Dact. Iam.
Tīme shăkes - thĕ stāblĕ - tȳrănny - ŏf thrōnes, &c
Whĕre ĭs - tŏmŏrrōw? - Ĭn ănŏth-ĕr wŏrld.
Shē āll - nīght lōng hĕr ăm-ŏrŏus dĕs-căn' sūng.
Innŭ mĕrāblĕ - bĕfōre - th' Almīgh ty's thrōne.
Thăt ŏn - wēak wĭngs - frŏm făr - pŭrsŭes - yŏur flĭght.

FIGURES OF SPEECH.

A figure of Speech is a mode of speaking, in which a word or sentence is to be understood in a sense different from its most common and literal meaning.

The principal Figures of Speech are,

Personification,	Sy-nec'do-che,
Simile,	Antithesis,
Metaphor,	Climax,
Allegory,	Exclamation,
Hy-per'bo-le,	Interrogation,
Irony,	Paralepsis,
Metonymy,	Apostrophe.

---

* *Iambus, trochee,* and *anapaest,* may be denominated *principal* feet because pieces of poetry may be wholly, or chiefly formed of any of them. The others may be termed *secondary,* because their chief use is to diversify the numbers, and to improve the verse.

Prosopopœia, or *Personification*, is that figure of speech by which we attribute life and action to inanimate objects; as, *The sea saw it and fled.*

A *simile* expresses the resemblance that one object bears to another; as, *He shall be like a tree planted by the rivers of water.*

A *metaphor* is a simile without the sign (like, or as, &c.) of comparison; as, *He shall be a tree planted by, &c.*

An *allegory* is a continuation of several metaphors, so connected in sense as to form a kind of parable or fable; thus, the people of Israel are represented under the image of a vine; *Thou hast brought a vine out of Egypt, &c.*, Ps. lxxx. 8 to 17.

An *hy-pĕr'-bō-lē* is a figure that represents things as greater or less, better or worse, than they really are; as, when David says of Saul and Jonathan, *They were swifter than eagles, they were stronger than lions.*

Irony is a figure by which we mean quite the contrary of what we say; as, when Elijah said to the worshippers of Baal, *Cry aloud for he is a god, &c.*

A *metonymy* is a figure by which we put the cause for the effect, or the effect for the cause; as, when we say, He reads *Milton;* we mean Milton's *Works. Grey hairs* should be respected, i. e. old age.

Synĕcdochē is the putting of a *part* for the *whole*, or the whole for a part, a definite number for an indefinite, &c.; as, The *waves* for the *sea*, the *head* for the *person*, and *ten thousand* for any great number. This figure is nearly allied to *metonymy*.

FIGURES OF SPEECH. 17

Antithesis, or *contrast*, is a figure by which different or contrary objects are contrasted, to make them show one another to advantage; thus, Solomon contrasts the timidity of the wicked with the courage of the righteous, when he says, *The wicked flee when no man pursueth, but the righteous are bold as a lion.*

* *Climax* is the heightening of all the circumstances of an object or action, which we wish to place in a strong light: as, *Who shall separate us from the love of Christ? Shall tribulation, or distress, or persecution, or famine, or nakedness, or peril, or sword? Nay, &c.*—See also, Rom. viii. 38, 39.

Exclamation is a figure that is used to express some strong emotion of the mind; as, *Oh the depth of the riches both of the wisdom and the knowledge of God!*

Interrogation is a figure by which we express the emotion of our mind, and enliven our discourse by proposing questions: thus, *Hath the Lord said it? and shall he not do it? Hath he spoken it? and shall he not make it good?*

Paralepsis or *omission*, is a figure by which the speaker pretends to conceal what he is really declaring and strongly enforcing; as, Horatius was once a very promising young gentleman, but in process of time he became so addicted to gaming, *not to mention his drunkenness and debauchery,* that he soon exhausted his estate and ruined his constitution.

Apostrophe is a turning off from the subject to address some other person or thing; as, *Death is swallowed up in victory: O death where is thy sting?*

---
* Climax, Amplification, Enumeration or Gradation.

Questions on the Text.

What is English Grammar?
Into how many parts is it divided?
What does *orthography* teach?
What is a *letter*, &c.?
Of what does *Etymology* treat?
How many parts of speech are there?

Article.

What is an *article*?
How many articles are there?
Where is *a* used?
Where is *an* used?

Noun—Number.

What is a *noun*?
How are nouns *varied*?
What is *number*?
How many *numbers* have nouns?
How is the *plural* generally formed?
How do nouns ending in *s, sh, ch, x,* or *o,* form the plural?
How do nouns in *y* form the plural?
How do nouns in *f* or *fe* form the plural?
What is the plural of *man,* &c.?

Gender.

What is meant by *gender*?
How many genders are there?
What does the *masculine* denote?
What does the *feminine* denote?
What does the *neuter* denote?
What is the feminine of bachelor, &c.?

Case.

What is *case*?
How many *cases* have nouns?
Which two are *alike*?
How is the possessive *singular* formed?
How is the possessive *plural* formed?
Decline the word *lady*. [ed]

Adjective.

What is an *adjective*?
How many *degrees* of *comparison* have adjectives?
How is the *comparative* formed?
How is the *superlative* formed?
How are dissyllables in *y* compared?
Compare the adjective *good*.

Pronouns.

What is a *pronoun*?
Which is the pronoun in the sentence, *He is a good boy*?
How many *kinds* of pronouns are there?
Decline the personal pronoun *I*.
Decline *thou* backwards, &c.

Relative Pronouns.

What is a *relative* pronoun?
What is the *rel.* in the example?
Which is the *antecedent*?
Repeat the relative pronouns.
Decline *who*.
How is *who* applied?
To what is *which* applied?
How is *that* used?
What sort of a relative is *what*?

Adjective Pronouns.

How many sorts of *adjective* pronouns are there?
Repeat the *possessive* pronouns.
Repeat the *distributive* pronouns
Repeat the *demonstrative*.
Repeat the *indefinite*.

On the Observations.

Before which of the vowels is *a* used?
What is *a* called?
What is *the* called?
In what sense is a noun taken *without* an *article* to limit it?
Is *a* used before nouns in both numbers?
How is *the* used?

Nouns.

How do nouns ending in *ch*, sounding *k*, form the plural?
How do nouns in *w*, &c., form the plural?
How do nouns ending in *ff* form the plural?
Repeat those nouns that do not change *f* or *fe* into *ves* in the plu
What do you mean by *proper* nouns?
What are *common* nouns?
What are *collective* nouns?
What do you call *abstract* nouns?

...tions on the Text and Observations.

Obs. Continued.

What do you call *verbal* nouns?
What nouns are generally *singular*?
Repeat some of those nouns that are used only in the *plural*.
Repeat some of those nouns that are *alike* in *both* numbers.
What is the singular of *sheep*?
What *gender* is *parent*, &c.?

Adjectives.

What does the *positive* express, &c.?
How are adjectives of *one* syllable generally compared?
How are adjectives of more than one syllable compared?
How are dissyllables ending with e final often compared?
Is y always changed into i before *er* and *est*?
How are *some* adjectives compared?
Do *all* adjectives admit of comparison?
How are *much* and *many* applied?
When is the final consonant *doubled* before adding *er* and *est*?

Relative Pronouns.

When are *who*, *which*, and *what* called *interrogatives*?
Of what *number* and *person* is the relative?

Adjective Pronouns.

When are *his* and *her* possessive pronouns?
What may *former* and *latter* be called?
When is *that* a *relative* pronoun?
When is *that* a *demonstrative*?
When is *that* a *conjunction*?
How many *cases* have *himself*, *herself*, &c.?

Verb.

What is a *verb*?
How many *kinds* of verbs are there?
What does a verb *active* express?
What does a verb *passive* express?
What does a verb *neuter* express?
Repeat the *auxiliary* verbs.
How is a verb *declined*?
How many *moods* have verbs?

Adverb.

What is an *adverb*?
Name the *adverbs* in the example.
What part of speech is the generality of those words that end in *ly*?
What part of speech are the compounds of *where*, *there*, &c.?
Are adverbs ever *compared*?
When are *more* and *most adjectives*, and when are they *adverbs*?

Preposition.

What is a *preposition*?
How many begin with *a*?
Repeat them.
How many begin with *b*?
Repeat them, &c.
What *case* does a preposition require after it?
When is *before* a preposition, and when is it an adverb?

Conjunction.

What is a *conjunction*?
How many *kinds* of conjunctions are there?
Repeat the *copulative*.
Repeat the *disjunctive*.

Interjection.

What is an *interjection*?

NOTE.—As these are only the *leading* questions on the different parts of speech, many more may be asked, "*viva voce*." Their distance from the answers will oblige the pupil to attend to the connection between every question and its respective answer. The observations that have no corresponding *question* are to be read, but not committed to memory.

FRENCH PHRASES.

As the following words and phrases, from the French and Latin, frequently occur in English authors, an explanation of them has been inserted here, for the convenience of those who are unacquainted with these languages. Let none, however, imagine, that by doing this I intend to encourage the use of them in English composition. On the contrary, I disapprove of it, and aver, that to express an idea in a foreign language, which can be expressed with equal perspicuity in our own, is not only pedantic, but highly improper. Such words and phrases, by being frequently used, may, notwithstanding the uncouthness of their sound and appearance, gradually incorporate with our language, and ultimately diminish its original excellence, and impair its native beauty.

Aide de-camp, * ād-de-kong`, *an assistant to a general.*
A la bonne heur, a la bon oor`, *luckily ; in good time.*
Affair de cœur, af-făr' de koor', *a love affair ; an amour.*
A la mode, a la mŏd`, *according to the fashion.*
A fin, a fing, *to the end.*
A propos, ap-prŏ-pŏ`, *to the purpose ; opportunely.*
Au fond, à fong`, *to the bottom, or main point.*
Auto da fé, à to-da-fā ; (*Portuguese*) *burning of heretics.*
Bagatelle, bag-a-tel`, *a trifle.*
Beau monde, bō mŏngd`, *the gay world, people of fashion.*
Beaux esprits, bōz es-prē, *men of wit.*
Billet doux, bil-le-dŭ`, *a love letter.*
Bon-mot, bong mŏ, *a piece of wit : a jest ; a quibble.*
Bon ton, bong tong, *in high fashion.*
Bon gré, mal gré, bong grā, &c., *with a good, or ill grace ; whether the party will or not.*
Bon jour, bong zhŭr, *good day ; good morning.*
Boudoir, bŭ-dwăr`, *a small private apartment.*
Carte blanche, kart blangsh`, *a blank ; unconditional terms*
Chateau, sha-tō`, *a country seat.*
Chef d'œuvre, she doo'ver, *a master-piece.*
Ci-devant, sē-de-vang`, *formerly.*
Comme il faut, com-il fō, *as it should be.*

Short vowels are left *unmarked* :—ŭ is equal to *u* in *rule* ;—ă to *a* in *art* ; oo, as used here, has no correspondent sound in English ; it is equal to *u*, as pronounced by the common people in many counties of Scotland, in the words *use, soot,* &c.—ā is equal to *a* in *all.*

* *A* is not exactly *a long* here ; it is perhaps as near *e* in *me* as *a* in *make,* but *a* will not be so readily mistaken. It is impossible to convey the pronunciation accurately without the tongue.

FRENCH PHRASES.

Con amore, con-a-mo're, (*Italian*) *with love ; with the partiality of affection.*
Congé d'elire, kong-zhā de-lēı , *leave to elect or choose.*
Coup de grace, kû-de gräss`, *a stroke of mercy; the finishing stroke.*
Coup d'œil, kû-dāil, *a peep ; a glance of the eye.*
Coup de main, kû-de-mäng`, *a sudden or bold enterprise.*
Debut, de-boo`, *first appearance in public.*
Dernier resort, dern'-yā-res-sor`, *the last shift or resource.*
Depot, dē-pō`, *a storehouse or magazine.*
Double entendre, dûbl ang-tang'der, *double meaning, one in an immodest sense.*
Douceur, dû-soor`, *a present or bribe.*
Dieu et mon droit, dyoo` e-mong-drwä, *God and my right.*
Eclat, e-klä, *splendour ; with applause.*
Elève, el äv`, *pupil.*
En bon point, ang-bong-pwang`, *in good condition ; jolly.*
En masse, ang mäss`, *in a body or mass.*
En passant, ang-pas-sang`, *by the way ; in passing ; by the by.*
Ennui, eng-nûē`, *wearisomeness ; lassitude ; tediousness.*
Faux pas, fō-pä, *a slip ; misconduct.*
Fête, fāt, *a feast or entertainment.*
Fracas, fra-cä`, *bustle ; a slight quarrel ; more ado about the thing than it is worth.*
Honi soit qui mal y pense, hō-nē-swä'kē-mäl ē pangs`, *evil be to him that evil thinks*
Hauteur, hâ-toor`, *haughtiness.*
Je ne sçais quoi, zhe ne sä kwä, *I know not what*
Jeu de mots, zhoo de mō`, *a play upon words.*
Jeu d'esprit, zhoo de-sprē`, *a display of wit ; a witticism.*
Mal-a propos, mal ap-ro-pō`, *unfit ; out of time or place.*
Mauvais honte, mo-väz-hōnt`, *false modesty.*
Mot du guét, mō doo gä`, *a watchword.*
Naïveté, na-iv-tā`, *ingenuousness, simplicity, innocence.*
Outré, û-trā`, *eccentric ; blustering ; wild ; not gentle.*
Petit maitre, pe-tē mā'ter, *a beau ; a fop.*
Protégé, pro-tā-zhā`, *a person patronized and protected.*
Rouge, rûzh, *red, or a kind of red paint for the face.*
Sans, sang, *without.*
Sans froid, sang frwä, *cold blood ; indifference.*
Savant, sa-vang, *a wise or learned man.*
Soi-disant, swä-dē-zang`, *self-styled ; pretended.*
Tapis, ta-pē, *the carpet.*
Trait, trā, *feature, touch, arrow, shaft.*
Tête a tête, tāt a tāt, *face to face, a private conversation.*
Unique, oo-nēk', *singular, the only one of his kind.*
Un bel esprit, oong bel e-sprē`, *a pretender to wit, a virtuoso.*
Valet-de-chambre, va-lā de shom'ber, *a valet or footman.*
Vive le roi, vēve le rwä, *long live the king.*

LATIN PHRASES.

The pronunciation has not been added to the Latin, because every letter is sounded,—e final being like y in army.

1. A *long* or *short* over a vowel denotes both the accented sylla ble and the *quantity* of the *vowel in English.*
2. Ti, ci, or si, before a vowel, sounds *she.*
3. Words of *two* syllables have he accent on the *first.*

Ab initio, *from the beginning.*
Ab urbe condita. *from the building of the city; abridged thus, A. U. C.*
Ad captandum vulgus, *to ensnare the vulgar.*
Ad infinitum, *to infinity, without end.*
Ad libitum, *at pleasure.*
Ad referendum. *for consideration.*
Ad valorem, *according to value.*
A fortiori, *with stronger reason, much more.*
Alias, (ā-le-as,) *otherwise.*
Alibi, (ăl-i-bi,) *elsewhere.*
Alma mater, *the university.*
Anglice, (ăng-gli-cv,) *in English.*
Anno Domini. *in the year of our Lord.—A. D.*
Anno Mundi. *in the year of the world.—A. M.*
A posteriori, *from the effect, from the latter, from behind.*
A priori, *from the former, from before, from the nature or cause.*
Arcanum, *a secret.*
Arcana imperii, *state secrets.*
Argumentum ad hominem. *on appeal to the professed principles or practices of the adversary.*
Argumentum ad judicium, *on appeal to the common sense of mankind.*
Argumentum ad fidem, *an appeal to our faith.*
Argumentum ad populum, *an appeal to the people.*
Argumentum ad passiones, *an appeal to the passions.*
Audi alteram partem, *hear both sides.*
Bona fide, *in reality, in good faith*
Contra, *against.*
Cacoethes scribendi, *an itch for writing.*
Ceteris (æ) paribus, *other circumstances being equal.*

Caput mortuum, *the worthless remains, dead head.*
Compos mentis, *in one's senses.*
Cum privilegio, *with privilege.*
Data, *things granted.*
De facto, *in fact, in reality.*
De jure, *in right, in law.*
Dei Gratia, *by the grace or favour of*
Deo volente, *God willing.* [God.
Desunt cætera, *the rest are wanting.*
Domine dirige nos, *O Lord, direct us.*
Desideratum, *something desirable, or much wanted.*
Dramatis personæ, *characters represented.*
Durante vita. *during life.*
Durante placito, *during pleasure*
Ergo, *therefore.*
Errata, *errors*—Erratum, *an error*
Excerpta, *extracts.*
Esto perpetua, *let it be perpetual*
Et cætera, *and the rest.* contr. &c
Exempli gratia, *as for example contracted, E. G.*
Ex officio, *officially, by virtue of office.*
Ex parte, *on one side.*
Ex tempore, *without premeditation.*
Fac simile, *exact copy or resemblance.*
Fiat, *let it be done or made*
Flagrante bello, *during hostilities.*
Gratis, *for nothing.*
Hora fugit, *the hour or time flies*
Humanum est errare, *to err is human.*
Ibidem, *in the same place,* contr. ib
Idem, *the same.*
Id est, *that is,* contracted, *i. e*
Ignoramus, *a vain uninformed pretender*

LATIN PHRASES.

In loco, in this place.
Imprimis, in the first place.
In terrorem, as a warning.
In propria persona, in his own person.
In statu quo, in the former state.
Ipse dixit, on his sole assertion.
Ipso facto, by the act itself.
Ipso jure, by the law itself.
Item, also or article.
Jure divino, by divine right.
Jure humano, by human law.
Jus gentium, the law of nations.
Locum tenens, deputy, substitute.
Labor omnia vincit, labour overcomes every thing.
Licentia vatum, a poetical license.
Lapsus linguæ, a slip of the tongue.
Magna charta, the great charter, the basis of our laws and liberties.
Memento mori, remember death.
Memorabilia, matters deserving of record.
Meum et tuum, mine and thine.
Multum in parvo, much in little, a great deal in few words.
Nemo me impune lacesset, no one shall provoke me with impunity.
Ne plus ultra, no farther, nothing beyond.
Nolens volens, willing or unwilling.
Non compos mentis, not of a sound mind.
Nisi Dominus frustra, unless the Lord be with us, all efforts are in vain.
Ne quid nimis, too much of one thing is good for nothing.
Nem. con. (for nemine contradicente,) none opposing.
Nem. dis. (for nemine dissentiente,) none disagreeing.
Ore tenus, from the mouth.
O tempora, O mores, O the times, O the manners.
Omnes, all.
Onus, burden.
Passim, every where.
Per se, by itself, alone.
Prima facie, at first view, or at first sight.
Posse comitatus, the power of the county
Primum mobile, the main spring.
Pro and con, for and against.

Pro bono publico, for the good of the public.
Pro loco et tempore, for the place and time.
Pro re nata, as occasion serv
Pro rege, lege, et grege; for the king, the constitution, and the people.
Quo animo, with what mind.
Quo jure, by what right.
Quoad, as far as.
Quondam, formerly.
Res publica, the commonwealth
Resurgam, I shall rise again.
Rex, a king.
Regina, a queen.
Senatus consultum, a decree of the senate.
Seriatim, in regular order.
Sine die, without specifying any particular day.
Sine qua non, an indispensable prerequisite or condition.
Statu quo, the state in which it was
Sub pœna, under a penalty.
Sui generis, the only one of his kind, singular.
Supra, above.
Summum bonum, the chief good.
Tria juncta in uno, three joined in one.
Toties quoties, as often as.
Una voce, with one voice, unanimously.
Ultimus, the last, (contracted ult.)
Utile dulce, the useful with the pleasant.
Uti possidetis, as ye possess, or present possession.
Verbatim, word for word.
Versus, against.
Vade mecum, go with me; a book fit for being a constant companion.
Vale, farewell.
Via, by the way of.
Vice, in the room of.
Vice versa, the reverse.
Vide, see, (contracted into v.)
Vide ut supra, see as above.
Vis poetica, poetic genius.
Viva voce, orally; by word of mouth
Vivant rex et regina, long live the king and the queen
Vox populi, the voice of the people,
Vulgo, commonly.

Index to the Rules of Syntax.

Nouns.

	Page
Two or more nouns in the singular,	83
Two nouns disjoined, &c.	ib.
Noun of multitude,	87
One noun governs another,	86
Of a clause between them,	109
Several nouns in the possessive,*	86
Singular nouns of diff. *persons*,	96
A *singular* and a *plural* noun,	97
A noun and its pron. improper,	99

Pronouns.

Pronouns agree in gender, &c.	93
Each, every, either, agree, &c.	106
That and this, former, latter,*	107
Relative agrees with its antec.	94
Relative *that* and *which*,†	ib.
Relative preceded by two antecedents of different persons,	95
Rel. should be placed next ant.	*ib.
Who after *than*,	*105
When a pronoun refers to *two* words of different *persons*,‡	97
Of *whichsoever*, &c.*	109

Verb

A verb agrees with its nom.	80
An active verb governs,	81
Neuter verbs do not govern an objective,‡	ib.
Active verbs admit of no preposition,‖	ib.
One verb governs another,	85
The infinitive is used as a nom.	99
Verbs related in point of time,	108
The verb *to be* has the same case,	88

Participle.

Participle used as a noun,	91
A possessive pronoun, before the present participle,	†91
A noun before the present participle,	19
Past Part. is used after *have* and *e*,	92

Adverbs.

	Page
Of the position of adverbs,	10*
Adjectives not used as adverbs,	10*
Of hence, thence, there, &c.*	ib.
Double comparatives improper,	10*
Two negatives improper,	10*
The comp. degree requires *than*,	10*

Prepositions.

Prepositions govern objective	82
——should be placed before the relative,*	82
Diff. preps. with the same noun,†	ib.
To, at, in, before names of places,	110
Words requiring appropriate prepositions,	111

Conjunctions.

Conjunctions couple like moods,	94
——require subjunctive mood,	89
Lest and that,†	ib.
If, with but following,†	ib.
Conjunctions in pairs,	90
——Than and as,	105

Various Things.

Interjections,	110
General Rule,	114
Use of the articles,	115
Ellipsis is frequently admitted,	11*
—— improper,	11*
Construction,	11*
Promiscuous Exercises on Syntax,	11*
Miscellaneous observations,	14*
When to use capitals,	15*
Prosody,	16*
Of versification,	ii*
Figures of speech,	16*
Questions on Etymology,	17*
French and Latin phrases,	17*

FINIS.

ADVERTISEMENT.

The preceding Grammar, owing to the uncommon precision and brevity of the Definitions, Rules, and Notes, is not only better adapted to the capacity of children than the generality of those styled Introductory Grammars, but it is so extensively provided with exercises of every sort, that it will entirely supersede the use of Mr. Murray's *Larger* Grammar and *Exercises*; for his is not a mere *outline*, like his *Abridgement*, which contains only about *seven* pages of exercises on *bad* Grammar. This contains more than *sixty*. This contains a *complete Course* of Grammar, and supersedes the use of any other book of the kind.

In short, by abridging every subject of minor importance; by omitting discussion on the numberless points about which grammarians differ; by rendering the rules and definitions more perspicuous, and at the same time abridging them more than *one-half*; by selecting short sentences on bad grammar; by leaving few broken lines, and printing them close together—as many exercises under each rule of syntax are compressed into this epitome as there are in Mr Murray's *volume of Exercises*; so that the use of his Abridgement, his larger Grammar, and that of his Exercises, are completely superseded by this little volume at 1s. 6d.; while, at the same time, the learner will acquire as much knowledge of grammar with this in *six* months, as with all these volumes in *twelve*.

The truth of this, as well as the unspeakable advantage of having the Grammar and Exercises in *one volume*, *teachers* will perceive at a glance; but as *parents* may not so quickly perceive the superior brevity and accuracy of the rules, it may not be improper to assist them a little, by comparing a few of the rules in this with those of Mr. Murray's; thus,

Mr Murray's Rules.	*Correspondent Rules in this.*
Rule II.—Two or more nouns, &c., in the singular number, joined together by a* copulative conjunction expressed or understood, must have verbs, nouns, and pronouns agreeing with them in the plural number; as, "Socrates and Plato *were* wise; *they* were the most eminent philosophers of Greece." "The sun that rolls over our heads, the food that we receive, the rest that we enjoy, daily *admonish* us of a superior and superintending power."—p. 143.	Rule IV.—Two or more singular nouns, coupled with *and* require a verb and pronoun in the plural number; as, James *and* John *are* good boys, for *they* are busy.—p 83.

---

* This rule is not only vague, but incorrect; for *a* means any one now any copulative conjunction will not combine the agency of two or more into *one*; none but *and* will do that.—Mr. M.'s *third* rule is equally vague.

Mr. Murray's Rules.	Corresponding Rules
Rule III.—The conjunction disjunctive has an effect contrary to that of the conjunction copulative; for, as the verb, noun, or pronoun, is referred to the preceding terms taken separately, it must be in the singular number; as, "Ignorance or negligence *has* caused this mistake;" "John, James, or Joseph, *intends* to accompany me;" "There *is* in many minds neither knowledge nor understanding."—p. 146.	Two or more singular nouns separated by *or* or *nor*, require a verb and pronoun in the singular; as, James *or* John *is* first.—p. 88
Rule IV.—A noun of multitude, or signifying many, may have a verb or pronoun agreeing with it, either of the singular or plural number; yet not without regard to the import of the word as conveying unity or plurality of idea; as, "The meeting *was* large;" "The Parliament *is* dissolved;" "The nation *is* powerful;" "My people *do* not consider; *they* have not known me;" "The multitude eagerly *pursue* pleasure as *their* chief good;" "The council *were* divided in *their* sentiments."—p. 147.	Rule VIII.—When a noun of multitude conveys *unity* of idea the verb and pronoun should be singular; as, The class *was* large. When a noun of multitude conveys *plurality* of idea, the verb and pronoun should be plural; as, My people *do* not consider; *they* have not known me.—p. 87
Rule XIX.—Some conjunctions require the indicative, some the subjunctive mood after them. It is a general rule, that when something contingent or doubtful is implied, the subjunctive ought to be used; as, "If I *were* to write, he would not regard it;" "He will not be pardoned *unless he repent.*" Conjunctions that are of a positive and absolute nature, require the indicative mood; "*As* virtue *advances*, so vice *recedes*;" "He is healthy, *because* he is temperate."—p. 193.	Rule X.—Sentences that imply contingency and futurity, require the subjunctive mood; as, *If* he be alone, give him the letter. When contingency and futurity are not implied, the indicative ought to be used; as, He speaks as he *thinks* he may safely be trusted.—p. 89.

---

* The second part of this rule is a flat contradiction of the first. The *first* says the verb and pronoun may be *either* of the singular or of plural number; the second says, *No*; "Not without regard to the import of the word," &c.

† It is easy to explain *contingency* and *futurity*, but what is a *positive* and *absolute* conjunction?

By the Author's Key to this Grammar, a grown-up person, though he had never learned Grammar before, may easily teach himself.

www.ingramcontent.com/pod-product-compliance
Lightning Source LLC
Chambersburg PA
CBHW020252170426
43202CB00008B/332